Oct 82

The Calendar of Organic Gardening

A Guidebook to Successful Gardening through the Year

by the editors of
Organic Gardening and Farming Magazine

edited by
Maurice Franz

Rodale Press, Inc. Book Division Emmaus, Pennsylvania 18049

Standard Book Number 0–87857–067–5

Library of Congress Card Number 73-2280

COPYRIGHT 1973 by RODALE PRESS, INC.

PRINTED IN THE UNITED STATES OF AMERICA

OB – 474

FOURTH PRINTING – FEBRUARY, 1975

Printed on Recycled Paper

Contents

Introduction
This Book Is the Work of Many Hands

It took more than 20 years to write this book which, in truth, is the work of many hands. From the pioneering days of Dr. William E. Eyster through the ministrations of Jerry A. Minnich and Betty Sudek down to the painstaking research of the late Dorothy Franz, much study and cumulative wisdom have been gathered from ever-widening horizons.

This material appeared originally in monthly issues of ORGANIC GARDENING AND FARMING. Over the years it constantly has been augmented and enhanced by the latest gardening developments, refined by practical experience and research both in the garden and laboratory.

The Calendar of Organic Gardening means to tell you how to garden day-by-day in seven different climate zones that stretch the length and breadth of our land, north to south and east to west—roughly 1,500 by 3,000 miles. From the very beginning it has been designed to help you garden better, working with the varieties that do best in your area, and using materials that are abundant—free wherever possible.

The book consists of 12 chapters, one for each month of the year—from January through December. Just as in OGF, each month is divided into five sections. The preliminary introduction states and focuses on the gardening situation or problem of the month. It is followed by four sections arranged according to their function as follows: The Vegetable Garden; The Ornamental Garden, The Orchard and Bush Fruits, and Under Glass.

There are no "mysteries" or "secrets" revealed breathlessly in *The Calendar of Organic Gardening*—only good gardening practices. Nor have we been interested in tricky short cuts;

we have tried instead to convey the all-embracing method of Organic Gardening as it progresses through the seasons and continues, indoors and out, for the full 12 months of the year.

One final word. Think of *The Calendar of Organic Gardening* as another tool out in the shed like your dibber, fork or hoe. Or your shredder and rotary tiller. Like them, it's been made to be used. So keep it handy and consult it, not only from time to time, but whenever a garden chore or operation is close at hand. We have so intended it that you'll find references to your tools on a continuing basis over the months. This *should give you a sense of the entire operation* and of the significance of the function you are performing at a given moment.

Yes. *The Calendar of Organic Gardening* is the work of many hands. But then, through the ages, gardening, itself, has been that way.

Maurice Franz

January
When Does Spring Start?

*The end of January is almost
in sight now, and for a full month,
the snow has been with us.*

The Twelve Seasons
Joseph Wood Krutch

January was not always the first month of the year. The Roman year originally began with March, and was ten months long. However, with time, January and February were added to the calendar, and by 251 B.C. January was accepted as the first month, although the other—and later—European nations did not adopt it as such until the 18th century. "Wulfmonath" was the Anglo-Saxon name for the first month, while March 25th marks the beginning of the ancient Jewish year, which date long held "a legal position in Christian countries as the opening of the new year," according to the *Encyclopedia Americana*.

It is more likely than not that the first planting, plowing or sowing marked, in ancient days, the first day of the new year. In Pennsylvania, Indians planted corn "when the leaf of the white oak was as large as a mouse's ear." The Greek poet Hesiod said that the time to plow and sow is when the cry

7

of migrating cranes is heard in the land. All of which indicates that March—not January—was once the first month of the year.

But although January definitely is the coldest—and now the first—month of the year, it heralds in a curious way the beginning of spring because we find ourselves worrying about what and when we can start to plant this year. Last year may have been a complete disaster in the vegetable patch and flower beds—but this year things will be different!

So we consult the seed catalogues, and our eyes stray to the frost zone maps, and we calculate ahead what we will plant, where we will plant it, and when. It's a good, common-sensical practice as long as we keep in mind that the zone map tells us more about *when* we can plant safely, than *what* we can plant, but those "growing days" between the frost dates dictate plainly when the planting will commence.

Now the number of frost-free days in the continental United States ranges from 260 near the Gulf of Mexico and in balmy California, to 100 in landlocked Minnesota and rock-bound Maine. And frosts can come at any time to the slopes of the Rockies—even in summer—so there can be no more than 80 frost-free growing days. Yet within these limitations, there are variations. Minnesota and Maine temperatures can sag to minus-40 in winter, while the mountain tops rarely get as cold as minus-30, which temperature is confidently expected in the Plains States where they enjoy 140 growing days.

So take another beginning-of-the-year look at the frost zone map inside the front cover. This is what it tries to tell you. In Zone One—there are a few scattered patches extending from northern Maine through upper Michigan to Wyoming and Idaho—the last spring frost may occur sometime in June. Zone Two can expect its last frost between May 10 and May 30. Three takes in possibly the greatest area, and can have frosts as late as April 10 and May 10. Zone Four, a skinny sort of geographical sliver that wanders from coast to coast, should see the end of frost sometime between March 20 and April 10. Zone Five—this is "Deep South" country— February 28 to March 10. Zone Six—February 8-28. Zone Seven—January 30 to February 8.

So, spring really starts now because you are looking ahead

to your planting schedule and operations again—thanks to the zone frost map.

Yes, although it's January, we're up to our ears in the spring planting and are even beginning to look ahead to beating the fall frosts.

But—one season at a time!

The Vegetable Garden

Be sure to plant something new this year along with your old favorites, now that the mailman's come with your seed and nursery catalogs. Be a bit extravagant in planning—the seeds don't cost much—because if you don't try a lot in gardening, you don't succeed with much!

Now's the time to run a germination test on any leftover seeds you plan to use. Sprinkle a few between damp blotters, and discard those that don't start to sprout in a reasonable period. Also start planning a 3- or 4-season garden ordering your seeds now for the first two seasons.

In planning your vegetable garden your first consideration should be family preferences. But even if your family does not like some of the more vitamin-rich greens, grow a few each year, and try to use them in new ways.

It is good practice to write the expiration date on each packet of seeds as it arrives. Some seeds lose viability quickly even when stored under ideal conditions. Onion seeds and members of this family should be ordered fresh each year. Lettuce, parsley, salsify, sweet corn and parsnips should all be planted within two years at most. Seeds that stay in good condition when kept dry for 3 to 5 years include asparagus, beans, cabbages, carrots, celery, chicory, endive, okra, peas, peppers, radishes, spinach and watermelon. Seeds good for 5 years or longer when kept dry and at room temperature are beets, cucumbers, muskmelons, mustard and tomatoes. Muskmelon seed has been known to germinate after 30 years in storage.

Seed potatoes should be ordered now by Zone Five gardeners. Or if you save your own, they should be set out now for greening. They sprout best on a window ledge that is warm and bright, but not sunny. It's also time to check your supplies of tomato, pepper, okra and eggplant seed against the offerings in the new catalogs, and get your orders in now, while preparing your hotbed and cold frame for next month's planting.

Plant round peas, onion plants and cabbages where the ground is workable. Perennial vegetables such as asparagus, rhubarb and horseradish may also be planted or transplanted this month.

In the milder Zone Three areas where the early narcissus bloom later in the month, peas and hardy root crops may be planted. It is not too late for residents in Zone Three and northward to manure the vegetable patch.

Peas, collards, kale and turnips may be planted at this time in the warmer, more southerly areas. The first potatoes can go in with reasonable safety where rain is normally scant. They may also be planted in the rainy areas on protected and well-drained hillsides. In the low, wet valleys, it is wiser to wait.

From North Carolina up along the Atlantic Coast it's not too late to spread manure over rows and patches. To prevent loss of nitrogen scatter the manure on top of the snow where it will sink in and benefit from later snows. Asparagus will especially prosper from a heavy cover of manure at this time.

The soil from South Carolina to the Gulf should be prepared for planting late this month and next month. In the warmer sections tomato seeds may be started in the open but should be covered with hotcaps. You should also be prepared to cover them with straw on a frosty night. Only the hardier plants should be started in the southern belt, and it is wiser and safer to wait until next month despite climatic blandishments. Strawberry plants and cabbages may be put out, but the cabbages should be covered with hotcaps in the colder sections.

Out on the foggy West Coast, artichoke beds may be started this month, with plenty of manure or compost dug deep into the bed. Set the roots six inches deep, and three to six feet apart. A well-prepared bed will last four or more years, but you can start a new bed every year, if you like, with suckers from the original plants. North of San Francisco, the bed should be protected with a good winter mulch.

Otherwise, the season may be started this month by planting garlic and onion sets, and seeds of kale, peas, collards and turnips. Tomato seeds may be started in the cold frame and a row or two of Irish potatoes should give you new potatoes for spring.

Save all the wood ashes from your fireplaces to use in next spring's fertilizer mixes, keeping them dry to preserve their potash content. Besides your fruit trees, the Irish potatoes will be more than grateful for an application—they need the potash to develop starches and sugars.

The Ornamental Garden

If you live in Zones Two or Three, uncover the cold frame on one of those unseasonably warm days that almost invariably arrives at this time, and sow primrose and rock garden Alpine seeds in the frame. Then, when the next snow falls, heap snow inside the frame. Seeds thus stratified will germinate in early spring.

On that same warm, sunny day, cut branches of pussy-willow and forsythia, and bring them indoors for forcing. Take care to select only the shoots that will not be missed when the shrubs bloom outside later. Put the shoots in water, and bring them into the living room so you can watch spring come early indoors.

This is also the month, farther south, when the tropical potted patio plants need protection. Make sure they don't get a chill by bringing them inside every night—if the tubs and planters have casters, it's easy to roll them along. Plants especially susceptible to cold include tropical palms such as licuala, red latan, and flowering trees and shrubs like frangipani, ixora, Hong Kong orchid and plumbago.

New Englanders and Middle Atlantic gardeners should check their stored bulbs and tubers, making sure they are not too dry. The sand around them should be damp to the touch. If the bulbs seem too wet, shift them to a drier spot, and inspect for signs of decay. The tender bulbs must be protected from freezing temperatures.

Stored plants of hydrangeas and azaleas should be started at this time for April bloom. An inside temperature of 50 degrees is recommended. The azaleas will need plenty of water right from the start, but the hydrangeas require little more water than is added to the leaves until they break out of the buds. As they develop, add more and more water to the plants.

Later in the month residents further west can sow such fine-seeded annuals as petunias, lobelia, snapdragon. Before germinating, some seeds require exposure to low temperatures and high moisture for a prolonged period.

During this dormant period in the moist soil, the seeds undergo a maturing or ripening period that is preliminary to actual germination. January is therefore a good month to start such plants as gentian, helleborus, pentstemon and aconite. Since they will not germinate for some weeks, sowing may be done outdoors in the open ground or indoors in pans or flats. If pans are used, sink them in the soil up to their rims.

This is a good month in the South for rose plantings which

should be dug in and set as soon as possible after they arrive. They do best in well-drained, slightly acid soil, particularly on a sunny site. For best results, be generous with compost in the planting hole.

Pruning can also begin at this time by cutting out all dead branches as well as the weaker stems. Bush roses in the South should not be cut back, however, to less than 18 inches, and the climber roses should not be pruned until they have finished blooming.

After setting your alyssum, candytuft, stocks, snapdragon and violas, plant lily and gladiolus bulbs among them, and broadcast some of the easier annuals such as larkspur, and poppies.

Fresh manure may be spread now on dormant peony beds, under shade trees and hedges, and in the shrubbery borders. Don't spread anywhere near bulb plantings. Otherwise and elsewhere, the manure will quickly soak in when spread on top of the snow while later snows will prevent nitrogen loss. Thaws and spring rains will leach the nutrients down to the root level in the spring—just when the plants need them most.

In the more arid sections of the Southwest, poppies should be planted at this time, and seeds of the iceplant and fig marigold should be started in the cold frame. Where conditions range from more humid to foggy, sow larkspur and sweet peas, and buy some pots of heather to plant in the garden.

The summer-blooming bulbs, such as anemones, ranunculus, gladiolus, amaryllis and ismene may be planted at lower elevations, for starting a succession for summer bloom. If you can find a dealer who will dig them at this time, try to add a few new lily hybrids.

In some sections daffodils may yet be planted. Empty flower beds in the northern Pacific coastal area should be sheet-composted now with manure and any other humus available. Subsequent rains will help break this material down into the soil in time for the spring plantings.

Are you a collector of discarded Christmas trees? If so, you can use them to advantage over the crowns of your hollyhocks, foxglove and delphiniums in addition to providing bird shelters (see "The Orchard and Bush Fruits"). If you have any leftover branches, use them to protect the south-facing parts of the rock garden.

Where the soil is frozen solid in northern regions around rhododendrons and mountain heaths, damage will be kept to a minimum if the tops of the plants are shaded and protected from the wind. Don't spread salt to melt ice on pavements or steps near the ornamental plantings. Sand will do the same job without damaging the plants.

The Orchard and Bush Fruits

Planting of all varieties of shade and fruit trees, shrubs and vines should be continued this month predominantly in the Zone Five area and south. If the ground is frozen early in the morning, wait until it thaws around midday. Finish pruning ornamentals, and prune the fruit trees and grapevines now before the February oil spraying.

Save pieces for cuttings as you prune the grapes. Best results come from pencil-thick lengths with two or three nodes spaced eight inches apart. Be sure to plant them right end up in the nursery. Mark the top with a slanting slice, and make the bottom end square with a straight cut. Space the cuttings three to four inches apart, and let them remain in the nursery for a full year before transplanting.

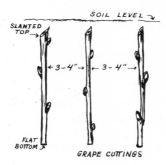

GRAPE CUTTINGS

If you live in Zones Five, Six, and Seven and wish to increase your stock of bramble fruits, dig up the roots of existing bushes to make cuttings. Pencil-thick cuttings, two to four inches long, are best. Sink them two inches deep in the cold frame until they sprout later in the spring when they should be transplanted in the nursery.

Some extra winter attention may be all that's needed to bring your old apple trees back into production. While they should not be pruned for another month in the colder areas, corky bark may now safely be scraped from their trunks and larger branches. It's good practice to catch the scrapings in a trap, and use them for tinder in the fireplace. When it's time to prune later, trim the old trees more drastically than the young ones. But don't try to do the entire job on a neglected tree at one session. It's better to remove one-third of the extra branches this year, another third next year, and so on. This way, you'll avoid excessive rain sprout development.

Fertilize as you prune. Each plant needs at least one bushel of compost, plus a pound or two of wood ashes and granite dust. Work the nutrients well into the soil before covering the entire root area with a fresh mulch of hay or shredded leaves. While taking care of the peaches, don't forget the figs and pecans.

Fruit trees and grapevines should also be pruned in the north Pacific coastal area, and also roses later in the month. While dormant all should be sprayed with miscible oil. Camellias suffering from tea scale should be sprayed with a very dilute oil emulsion.

Orange, lemon, tangerine and grapefruit trees can now be planted in Zones Six and Seven. All of these love plenty of humus and hate wet feet, so if you're in doubt about drainage, plant each tree in a hill built up like a pitcher's mound.

Manure should be spread at this time under fruit and nut trees. Grapes should be pruned and cuttings set in the home nursery just as described above for Zone Five residents. The cuttings should be ready within a year to expand the present vineyard or replace damaged vines.

Trees and shrubs can also be planted late this month in the central states where the soil is open and not too wet. Fruit and nut trees and grapevines should be pruned either on a warm day late in the month or in February. Save cuttings from the trees for spring grafting, tieing them in bundles and burying them in a cold frame or in a basket of moist sawdust in the root cellar. Grapevine cuttings may be treated in the same way, or planted immediately in the cold frame. The summer-blooming shrubs should also be pruned now.

After the pruning is done, give the trees and shrubs their dormant oil spraying. Make your own miscible oil mixture if you have a lot of spraying to do. Heat together two parts of a light-grade (#10) oil with one part of fish-oil soap, pouring the mixture from one container into another, back and forth, until the mixture emulsifies. Dilute with 20 times its volume of water and use quickly before it separates. Dilute in twice as much water when spraying evergreens.

Read the label carefully before buying any commercial miscible sprays. Many of the commercial products contain poisonous materials that can kill off healthy soil life and remain in the soil for years.

Orange trees should be planted this month or in February. Unless the planting weather is quite humid, buy balled and burlapped stock. Give the trees a site in the full sun where they will be sheltered from strong, drying winds. Where drainage is a problem, build a mound of rich humus in which to plant the trees. Two Navel and two Valencias will keep a family supplied all year.

Fruit trees should be inspected on the warmer days for masses of eggs and cocoons which should be destroyed—burning is advisable unless your compost pile really heats up to the 135-degree mark. But be careful to spare the eggs of praying mantis—silvery and spindle-shaped, about two inches long, and spun around stems or twigs.

Inspect the trunks of peach and apple trees for borers. If you find a trickle of sawdust, look above for the hole where the insect entered. Slit the bark straight down from the hole, following the tunnel until you overtake and destroy the pest.

Don't forget the birds. Keep their feeding trays and boxes full in all weather! They may need your help during a heavy snowstorm, and you can make a serviceable shelter out of discarded Christmas trees tied together at the top to form a tepee that is open to the south.

Under Glass

January is a critical month in the greenhouse and cold frame. You don't have to be concerned, despite appearances, about the plants in the frame when there is a good covering of snow. But if you're having an open winter, or there is a thaw—take care! Keep those burlap bags, old tarps and blankets handy if you don't have a good supply of hay or straw. It is the rapid rise and fall of temperature that, unchecked by a protective layer, encourages the appearance of fungus infections.

Are your hotbeds insulated by now? If not, it's high time you began to protect their residents against those stone-cold nights that are sure to arrive tonight—or tomorrow. Fill your burlap or plastic sacks with straw or hay and spread them over the glass of each hotbed at sundown. Cover the glass thoroughly with the sacks held in position with a tarpaulin, or old blankets or bedspreads. Under such a cover even the tallest lettuce leaves will escape frostbite even when they reach up to touch the glass.

On the window sills, bring the cool-exposure plants from the north side of the house to the east windows while allowing the plants from the east more sun on the south. Also, give the foliage planters that usually are set on the tables away from the primary light a short midwinter visit to one of the less exposed windows.

Since the extra cold nights that prevail in January and February can be dangerous to plants too close to the glass both in the greenhouse or on the windowsill, draw the drapes at night or slip lengths of protective cardboard between the plants and the glass. Despite all precautions, move the tenderest plants away from the window on the coldest nights.

Check the temperature gauges and controls to make sure your heating system is working at top efficiency. In case of a power failure, bring back the heat slowly, raising it first to about 35 degrees, then to 40 in about one hour, and so on until things are normal again. While you're doing this, also be sure to wet down the plants thoroughly with a very fine mist or spray, keeping them moist as the temperature rises. This will help keep damage to a minimum and actually save many plants that would otherwise be lost.

Be sure that the plants in the greenhouse and hotbed have enough room to breathe and spread out. Crowding can lead to vexing trouble in the middle of winter when the ventilators are so rarely opened. The still, rather damp air encourages fungus disease infection, and the soft growth made by the indoor plants invites aphid infestation—particularly when crowding occurs.

Introduce all gifts into the greenhouse only after a thorough check for insects and signs of disease. This is the month to be on the alert for infected plants which should be removed immediately when discovered. Don't overwater, and feed sparingly while plant growth is slowed.

If you can find the room, try to keep all new plants separate for ten days to two weeks—a shelf or area at least 12 inches away from any other plant is fine.

Remove all foil wrappings from pots as soon as possible, and set the plants where the day temperature is well below 70 degrees, and between 55 and 60 degrees at night. Although bright shade will be needed to bring buds into bloom, strong sunlight and drafts should be avoided.

Keep watering to a minimum this month—overwatering encourages fungi. Water only when the soil is dry to the touch or the foliage of the large-leaved plants is obviously drooping. Try to avoid splattering or splashing the leaves. But wetting down the walks and under the benches will help maintain the proper humidity.

Feeding, except where you're deliberately forcing, should also be kept to a minimum. Most plant growth is now at its lowest, and the food needs are correspondingly minimal. As a rule, organic fertilizers are taken up rather slowly when the temperature is below 60 degrees.

Temperature of the water is one of the most important factors in the successful care of African violets—it should always be room temperature or warmer. Also, water from the bottom and do not wet the leaves.

Now that the holidays are safely past, this is a good time for the mid-winter clean-up. Algae should be scrubbed off the benches, pots, windows and sills with warm water and vinegar. Remove the dust from your house plants, using the softest brushes you have for the African violets and episcias. Ferns can be turned over, and their tops swished in a pot of water, adding some soap to the water for the ivy. The other plants will appreciate a soft shower in the bathroom or kitchen sink.

Branches of forsythia, pussy willow and dogwood can be forced now. When the weather is right for pruning, bring in some lopped-off apple, cherry and peach boughs. While the colors of fruit blossoms are somewhat disappointing when forced, they keep alive our hopes of how soon we will be enjoying real spring blossoms.

Potted daffodils and single tulips can be brought in now from the cold frame for forcing. Keep them in cool shade either in the greenhouse or on a windowsill until growth is one inch high; then transfer them to a sunny spot. Do not overwater them before they show a good leaf growth.

In Zones Four and Five, start the following seeds indoors for transplanting later to the garden: lettuce, kale, beets and turnips. Tomatoes should also be started in Zone Five, and in Zones Six and Seven start them outside under hotcaps. West Coast gardeners can also start begonias and streptocarpus in pots from seed.

Christmas poinsettias may be treated like cut flowers and discarded when their bloom fails. Or they may be carried over for possible bloom next year. Unless you have greenhouse equipment it's wiser to discard; it takes a lot of fussing to bring them into bloom another year. This also applies to Christmas begonias, cyclamen and heather.

February
A Word About Seeds

O, little is my garden space,
But great the prayer I pray;
With every seed against earth's need
That men may sow today,
My hope is thrown, my faith is sown
To make the harvest gay.

A Prayer At Planting Time
Theodosia Garrison

February may be an "off" gardening month to some folks—but we don't see it that way at all. What you do at this time can make or break your gardening program and activities for the rest of the year.

So we're proposing in this "off" month to make a study of the seeds that men sow "against earth's need." We want to know more about what we are doing—and why we do it—when the time comes to plant them next month, and the month after that, and the months after that. We are concerned here with the time it takes for seeds to germinate, the time it takes for the plants to achieve successful and fruitful maturity, and the soil temperatures the various seeds and plants require.

A working knowledge of these factors will enable you to get your gardening program started indoors on a practical schedule, moving your plants outdoors as local weather conditions and the various plants' own needs permit. A program, thus maintained, will permit successive crops and double harvests that should fill your freezer and cellar shelves next winter. And, one factor more, bear in mind that plants that are given a good start and come to early maturity are better able to withstand insect attacks and midsummer dry weather —they're stronger and their roots are down deeper.

Vegetable seeds and their soil requirements for successful germination and fruitful maturity may be divided into three broad categories: 1—those that require cool soil; 2—those that tolerate cool soil; 3—those that require warm soil. Understanding these groups and their needs will obviously make us all better gardeners, and a little study in this "off" gardening month should bring its rewards later in the "on" months in the form of greater yields.

In the following list are the temperature ranges and germination and maturity times for plants whose seeds need cool soil.

Celeriac: 50-68 degrees, 10-21 days. Celery: 50-68 degrees, 10-21 days, 80-102 days from transplanting to maturity. Leek: 68 degrees, 6-14 days, 130-150 days maturity. Lettuce: 68 degrees, 7 days, 45 days transplanting to maturity for leaf varieties and 75-85 days for head lettuce. Onions: 68 degrees, 6-10 days, 100-125 days field seeding to harvest. Peas: 68 degrees, 5-8 days, 55-70 days field seeding. Radish: 68 degrees, 4-6 days germination, 23-25 days maturity. Salsify: 68 degrees, 5-10 days, 150 days maturity. Spinach: 59 degrees, 7-21 days, 42-50 days maturity. —New Zealand: 50-86 degrees, 5-28 days, 70 days maturity.

Cool-soil tolerant seeds and plants do best with a temperature range of 68-86 degrees and comprise the most numerous and productive vegetable group. Without these nutritious, vitamin-packed crops our diets would be meager indeed, and our gardens greatly reduced in scope.

Beets: 3-14 days germination, 55-65 days from field seeding

to maturity. Broccoli: 3-10 days, 60-75 days from transplanting. Brussels Sprouts: 3-10 days, 90 days from transplanting. Cabbage: 3-10 days, 65-100 days from transplanting. —Chinese: 3-7 days, 70-75 days. Carrots: 6-21 days, 65-75 days field seeding. Cauliflower: 3-10 days, 58-65 days from transplanting. Chard, Swiss: 3-14 days, 60 days maturity. Collards: 3-10 days, 80 days maturity. Cornsalad: 7-28 days, 60 days maturity. Cress: 4-10 days, light-sensitive. —Water: 4-14 days, 50 days maturity. Endive: 5-14 days, 65-90 days maturity. Kale: 3-10 days, 55-65 days maturity. Kohlrabi: 3-10 days, 55-60 days. Mustard: 3-7 days, 35-50 days. Parsley: 11-28 days, 70-90 days. Parsnips: 6-28 days, 95-105 days. Rutabaga: 3-14 days, 90 days. Turnip: 3-7 days, 45-70 days.

The vegetable group that is most productive when soil temperatures are in the upper range includes some of the most popular and universally desired foods—the bean family, corn, melons and pumpkins. Germination of seeds takes place between 68 and 86 degrees, but the aware gardener will proceed carefully and thoughtfully when the time comes either to start these crops outdoors or to move them to their permanent planting sites. A hasty move or one bad night can undo a lot of laborious and time-consuming work.

Beans, Pole: 5-8 days, 60-70 days maturity. —Lima: 5-9 days, 65-90 days. —Snap: 5-9 days, 48-56 days. Corn: 4-7 days, 65-90 days. Cowpeas: 5-8 days, 60 days. Cucumber: 3-7 days, 52-62 days. Eggplant: 7-14 days, 80-85 days transplanting to maturity. Muskmelon: 4-10 days, 80-90 days. Okra: 4-14 days, 50-56 days. Pepper: 6-14 days, 60-75 days. Pumpkin: 4-6 days, 100-120 days. Soybean: 5-8 days, 96 days. Squash, Summer: 4-7 days, 50-60 days. —Fall: 4-7 days, 85-120 days. Tomato: 5-14 days, 65-85 days.

In conclusion, we would like to suggest that you hold on to the plant groupings presented here according to seed requirements, referring to them when making up your garden plans for the next eight months. Maybe February is an "off" month in a gardening sense. But when we consider it from *The Calendar of Organic Gardening* angle, it takes on a new and different aspect. What you plan—and start—in February makes it an "on," if not an "in" gardening month.

The Vegetable Garden

Is fresh manure plentiful in your area? According to the agricultural reports, it is overabundant in many parts of the country, where it is considered a threat to groundwater supplies. To help relieve a possible organic glut in your area, and raise earlier crops, plan to operate a manure hotbed in time for the spring planting by drawing upon the local dairy farms for a bountiful supply of the freshest-possible manure.

Turn the pile every two or three days before you build the bed. Next, spread and tramp down a layer of manure 15 to 24 inches thick at the bottom of the hotbed pit. Cover this with four to six inches of sifted soil, then permit to heat up and then cool before planting.

This is also the time to prepare the beds for the strawberries or asparagus you plan to start in March. Be sure to enrich both with rock fertilizer and a generous application of compost. The top six inches of the strawberry bed should get most of the fertilizers, but you should double-dig the asparagus bed, going at least 12 inches down and replacing the lower level with good topsoil mixed with bone meal.

Out on the West Coast, in the southern areas, asparagus can be sown now until the end of March. Mix the seed with 15 times its bulk in sand for the best germination, and place in a cloth-lined container or pot. Pour warm water through the seeds two or three times a day for two days, then keep in a moist condition until sprouting begins—usually within a week. Sprinkle sand and sprouted seed over the surface of a well-prepared bed and sift 1-1/2 inches of fine soil over the seed.

Keep the bed moist until the seedlings have sent out deep roots. The seed may be sown on the permanent site or in a nursery bed. If the former, keep the weeds under firm control until the top of the young plants are bushy. If you have planted in the nursery, the roots will have to be dug next November and transferred to a permanent site.

Otherwise, outdoor vegetable gardening begins this month only in Zones Four through Seven. North of that area, all vegetable planting will take place under glass.

The first pale shoots of sea kale will come up either this month or next. Watch for them, and when they appear heap a foot-high mound of soil over them. When they make their way through the mound and poke their curly tips up again, dig away the dirt, and reap the first vegetable crop of the new season!

Vegetables that should be started now indoors are listed in the "Under Glass" section. The outdoor vegetable season will begin this month only in Zones Four through Seven.

In the southern sector of Zone Four and south, rhubarb and asparagus roots, onion and spinach seed and cabbage plants can go in now. In Zones Five and Six, seed may also be sown outdoors for Brussels sprouts, carrots, cauliflower, chard, chervil, chives, collards, cress, dandelions, kale, leaf lettuce, leeks, mustard, parsley, parsnips, turnips, peas, potatoes, salsify and sorrel. Horseradish roots, onion sets and head lettuce plants may also be set out. As soon as the ground can be worked in Zone Four, corn salad, garlic, peas and spinach may be sown.

Turn under cover crops and weeds in all areas as soon as the soil is open so that they will break down before planting time. If you're not too far north, and particularly in an area afflicted by drought, apply mulch as soon as the soil is turned. Otherwise, from Zone Three upward, you'll do better to keep the mulch away from the rows for one or two weeks to give the soil a chance to really warm up.

Should you have any finished compost left over, use generous amounts of it as you prepare the garden rows for planting. Thoroughly turn and aerate the compost piles you have been building all winter, particularly if you have been including the family garbage. Start new heaps at the same time, using manure, more kitchen wastes, shredded leaves and clippings. The new compost should be ready for use at midsummer planting time.

If the weather comes on warm and dry this year, gardeners in the Central States may get the chance to rotary-till a few rows, getting them ready for planting. If the soil is advanced enough and the tiller is up to the chore, you can get a real head start by tilling under plenty of finished compost and aged manure. Leave rough when you turn under the sheet compost and cover crops on areas that will be planted in April.

Green peas may be planted even in Zone Two areas provided you sheet composted in the fall, and turned under a good supply of soil nutrients and conditioners. Loss from leaching is small when the soil freezes and the cold inhibits soil life and functions.

Wait for a warm spell that loosens the very top, scrape aside the winter mulch cover and plant your seeds in a shallow drill, covering them with about one inch of soil. It's good practice to include nitrogen-fixing inoculants with the seeds in the rows. Such early planting of early peas should give you a well-prepared planting patch for your corn in early summer after you turn the pea foliage under.

Warm up your shredder on one of the balmier days— putting in fresh, warm engine oil helps loosen its frost-slowed joints—and put it to work on the pile of leaves you stashed away in an enclosure last fall. The chopped-up, easily-handled particles can be spread over the planting rows and subsequently turned under, added to the compost pile, or used as mulch as your plants advance with the season.

The Ornamental Garden

It's time, in Zones Two and Three, to start removing the mulch from the spring-flowering bulb beds so the soil can start warming up. Sprinkle bone meal and compost generously around all hardy bulbs as soon as their first shoots appear, particularly those that have been in the ground for one year or more.

Up in Zones Two and Three, sweet peas and other hardy annuals may be planted outdoors—providing the weather is agreeable. Most gardeners who rate Washington's birthday as the most propitious day for planting sweet peas advance-prepare the sowing trench in the fall so it is ready for seeds in the early spring.

Stuff plenty of compost in the bottom to within five inches of the top, and plant the seeds about one inch apart, covering them with about one inch of soil. Keep filling the trench with soil as the young plants grow, until it is level with the surface of the ground. Plants with these deep roots will be less likely to dry out over the summer, and should give you long bloom.

It's advisable, in Zones One and Two, to check perennials for heaving as soon as the snow melts, or the wind blows the ground clear near the beds and borders. Where damage is evident, cover the affected plants with straw or evergreen branches to prevent more damage after pressing the roots back into the earth as gently as possible.

Dahlias, begonias, lobelia and petunias may be sown now in protected or heated frames. The hardy perennials can be planted in cold frames or protected open sites, and the hardy annuals may also be started.

Somewhat west, in the predominantly Zone Three area, try sowing cascade chrysanthemum seeds to enhance your walls, lattices, hanging baskets, terraces and pergolas. Plant them in humus-rich soil in small pots, and when they are about one foot high, pinch everything back to one inch—except for the strongest stem. Tie the shoot to a wood or wire support set at an angle, keeping the side shoots pinched off.

After the buds form, lower the support gradually until it is in a horizontal position. Eventually, it should be removed completely, and the plant allowed to cascade with three-foot flowering stems that can remain covered with blooms for as much as two months, if you keep it in the shade.

To make sure you get a good array of fall-flowering chrysanthemums, take up the old plants, divide them and replant in fresh soil. Although they are perennials, chrysanthemums will reward you with extra-lovely flowers when divided and replanted each year.

The following may be set out before the end of the month in Zones Five, Six and Seven: ageratum, alyssum, anchusa, snapdragon, daisy, pinks, gerbera, carnation, Chinese forget-me-not, petunias, phlox, stocks, violas and sweet william.

Gardeners in the Southeast, primarily those in Zone Five and some favored spots in Zone Four, may begin—at the end of the month—to wash away the soil that has mounded over the tender tea roses. Then leave the beds open to the sun for four to six weeks before applying mulch.

Cut back part of the winter-blooming annuals in Zones Six and Seven to encourage new growth which should bloom after the main blossoming is over. It should help your garden bridge the gap between the winter and spring flowers. It's also time to assess your ornamentals now and order trees and shrubs to brighten next winter's garden.

Roses will still be dormant further West and so may be planted at this time. Pick a spot where drainage is really adequate to dig a deep bed, and be sure to add plenty of humus to the soil. Give the young plants plenty of potash rock, but be sparing with the nitrogen.

If the soil is sandy, set the plants deep enough to almost cover the bud graft. But if the soil is adobe leave the graft well-exposed. Work preferably with heat-resistant varieties if you live in a low area.

Roses may be pruned now in Zone Seven, and the mulch removed. As noted above, the soil should be left bare before you spread fresh mulch. This is the last rose-planting month in this area although operations may be delayed somewhat in Zone Six until the end of the month. But the new bushes should be planted now, if possible.

Since some rosa rugosa varieties have been found that can withstand temperatures down to minus-thirty (-30), gardeners in the coldest parts of Zones One and Two need no longer hesitate to plant these ornamentals that bear vitamin-C fruits so abundantly. Order now for dormant plants that will be delivered when the snow is off the ground.

Hansa is recommended for hardiness; for beauty and yield plant Blanc Double De Coubert, Frau Dagmar Hartopp, Nova Zembla, Sarah Van Fleet, Dr. Eckener, Amelie Garvereaux, Flamingo, Ruskin and Sanguinaire. If you want to propagate any of the above varieties in your home nursery, take softwood cuttings next summer, or hardwood cuttings late in the fall. Being hybrids, they cannot be propagated from seed.

On the West Coast it's time to start loosening the mulch around the early-blooming perennials and bulbs. Other flowers that may be seeded now in flats include dahlia, ageratum, lobelia, scabiosa, snapdragon and verbena. In Zones Six and Seven, cut back on part of the winter-blooming annuals after the main show is over to encourage new growth for bloom— it helps bridge the dun and dull time between winter and spring. Summer bulbs that may be planted now include gladiolas, amaryllis and ismene.

Above all, start a garden diary this month and then keep at it. Don't be afraid to make diagrams that show the kinds and positions of the various species and varieties. Be sure to keep records of sowing and planting dates, the length of time elapsed before first appearance, also the dates of transplanting and blooming.

Don't neglect to jot down any other facts or characteristics that appear significant. Such notes can be of great value and pleasure in future years, guiding and rewarding you at the same time. Just remember the centuries-old records kept in the abbeys of England and France as well as the vineyards of western Europe! Heights of plants, times and duration of bloom can help you obtain and maintain future garden success. This, as always, is a good year to start your garden diary.

The Orchard and Bush Fruits

As soon as the soil is open, pick a dark, cold mizzly day for transplanting trees and shrubs from your home nursery. The more miserable the weather (and you) the better for your young transplants.

Otherwise, February, in Zones Four through Seven, is one of the best grape-planting months of the year. In the eastern parts where winters are only reasonably cold—never below minus-five—the following Concords are recommended: Delaware, Portland, Niagara and Brockton. Not so hardy, Extra and Athens cannot stand temperatures below five degrees which puts them in the same class as the muscadines.

Among these, the Scuppernongs are particularly esteemed for their high vitamin C content. The western viniferas are mostly tender below 15 degrees, and do not do well where coastal fogs roll inland. In very hot valleys, plant Red Málaga and Emperor. The Frame Tokays will ripen well in the cool valleys, so will Ribier, Lady Fingers, Thompson Seedless and Muscat.

In Zones Five through Seven, pomegranates and Japanese persimmons make good ornamental plants in small home gardens. They are fairly hardy once they become established, although they may not bear a crop every year in all sections of the South. They should be planted this month before they come into bloom.

Zones Six and Seven orchardists should plant their citrus stock now. It's good practice to order your trees balled, burlapped and certified, if possible.

After each storm, examine your trees, and cut back all damaged limbs before they break and tear back, injuring the bark. Residents in Zones One and Two can start pruning their fruit trees and grapevines, providing the weather really warms up. But you're advised not to rush the job if March comes on strong in your area, with lots of winter still in store. It's a pleasant custom to save the best prunings from the apple and peach trees for forcing indoors—their white blooms brighten the house and provide a welcome token that heralds the coming of spring.

As soon as the coldest weather is past in your area, start pruning your fruit trees. The grape vines can wait until after the trees are pruned, but the berry bushes should also be pruned now if the job was neglected last summer. The raspberry canes should be cut back by one-third. After pruning, give each plant its dormant oil spraying, plus its spring nitrogen-rich fertilizer consisting of manure, tankage, cottonseed meal or bone meal.

The annual fruit-tree and shrub pruning further south should be finished just before the last frost. Go slow with the frostbitten limbs—give them a chance to revive before cutting them back, although it may take several months. Otherwise, finish planting of all dormant trees and shrubs; be sure to set them out before their buds begin to swell. Again, give all your trees their annual nitrogen feeding if you have not done so already.

Meanwhile, you can take full advantage of the dormant season by planting out your trees and shrubs. Get them into the ground before the buds begin to swell. At the same time, give all your trees and woody growths their annual feeding of organic nitrogen fertilizer if you haven't already done so.

Homesteaders in the Southwest should continue to plant out both their evergreen and deciduous ornamentals until the end of the month. If your area really suffers from drought, work with arid-tolerant desert plants and drought-resistant exotics which should free your water reserves for the fruits and vegetables which may really need help.

Central State residents in Zone Three will find it pays now to check their trees for tent caterpillar eggs. They look like gobs of chewing gum mixed with sand, and are usually found on small branches or twigs. But when getting rid of them, watch out for the spindle-shaped, paper cocoons that protect the praying mantis. These are silvery and spun around the branches of shrubs and low trees.

If you have not already ordered all the new bush and tree fruit stock you mean to buy this year—do it now. It somehow spoils the fun when you have to endure the disappointment of the nurseryman's attached note: "Sorry, all sold out—may we substitute?" So don't get caught with a patched-over orchard program because all the choice varieties were sold.

Don't forget our feathered friends at the very end of winter. Keep plenty of wild birdseed handy for that last blizzard that always arrives when we don't need it. If you're out in the country, provide your 4-footed neighbors with a handout of dried corn, carrot tops, and bruised apples that were headed for the compost pile. If you leave food near their runs, they may reward you by not nibbling the bark off your tender young fruit trees.

Under Glass

Vegetables that can be started in the first half of the month include celery, parsley and Spanish onions. Later it's time for the early cabbages, peppers, tomatoes, broccoli, cauliflower, eggplant, endive, kohlrabi and leeks. This is also the time for the last plantings of Bibb lettuce and radishes.

Crops that should be started now under glass or outdoors with protection in Zones Four and Five include Brussels sprouts and Malabar spinach which should be planted before the end of the month in Zone Three. Peppers and tomatoes may be sown indoors in Zone Four around Washington's birthday.

Include some head lettuce seed when you do your green-house planting so you will have large plants ready for setting out in the spring.

Onion seed planted now in the hotbed or greenhouse, will give you an early crop of scallions. The leftovers can later be transferred to outdoor rows for early bulbs.

From Zone Four north, the following flowers can be sowed indoors for later transplanting to the outdoors—asters, petunias, lobelia, lantana, flowering tobacco, stocks, nemesia, snap-dragon, Shasta daisies, Canterbury bells and cup-and-saucer vine.

The seeds of many annuals should be sown this month to produce blooming-size plants for the May garden. The finer seeds, such as lobelia, petunia and flowering tobacco should be scattered evenly over the surface without being covered. The larger-seeded plants may also be scattered or sown in rows but should be covered with 1/8-inch of soil. A four-inch pot is adequate for a few seeds; a flat will be necessary for larger sowings.

After the seed has been sown and the planting mixture watered—preferably from below—the pot or flat should be covered with glass or pliable plastic. Bottom heat, ranging from 60 to 65 degrees, will aid germination. Raise a corner of the cover when the seedlings begin to appear; follow this by exposing them completely in three or four days. Water with a fine spray of slightly warm water as needed, and when the plants are large enough, transfer them.

Annuals that should thrive under this regimen include ageratum, asters, candytuft, coleus, annual dahlias, early bloom-ing poppy, stocks, sweet william, verbena and zinnia for early blooms.

The half-hardy annuals may be started now in Zones Five and Six to be set out after the very last frosts. Safely included among these are zinnias, sunflowers, castor bean, celosia, Job's tears, crotalaria, brachycome, salpiglossis, schizanthus, amar-anthus, martynia and torenia.

Perennials that should be sown for the outdoor garden in-clude aconite, aquilegia, campanula, delphinium, oriental poppy, pyrethrum, trollius and viola.

It's not too late for Zone Two gardeners to plant seed now that calls for stratification. After sowing the seeds in flats or protected cold frames, expose the planting sites to freezing and snow.

December and January cuttings should be shifted to two or three-inch pots when the roots are one-half to one-inch long. They should be thoroughly watered immediately after potting, and then only watered sparingly for a few days. Feed with liquid fish fertilizer (one tablespoon to one gallon of water) every two or three weeks.

Rooted cuttings of chrysanthemums should be ready for potting in about three weeks. Set a group of three in a five-to-six-inch pan for bloom in April and May, and pinch every three weeks until mid-March to stimulate side-branching. To prevent too-early blooming, keep the lights on for the first few weeks.

It's time to transfer seedlings to pots and flats or to the bench as they grow and are easy to handle. Use a general soil mixture. Youngsters which may be set in the bench include: calendula—six to eight inches apart; chrysanthemums (annual types)—six to eight inches; larkspur—four inches; marigolds—six inches; salpiglossis—six inches. Gazanias should be transferred at first to two-inch pots, later to four-inch pots. Thin godetia six to nine per pot, and provide some support. Vinca rosea should go straight into three-inch pots since they do not transplant well from flats.

For best results with African violets started at this time from seed, keep in a humid environment, preferably under glass, using a covered butter, fruit or vegetable dish. The growing mixture—ground peat moss and sand—should be quite wet, but not soggy. Scatter the very fine seed over the surface as evenly as possible, and fit the cover over the container. Keep the seeds in the light with 70 to 75 degrees bottom heat. When the seedlings are about one inch tall, shift them to flats or individual two-inch pots.

Begonia tubers may be taken from their old pots now and cleaned. Spread them out on a board in the cellar or a darkened room, and sprinkle with water every other day. When they start to sprout, place them on a bed of wet peat or sphagnum moss, and allow the sprouts to grow several inches before potting them in soil rich with compost.

Don't neglect the house plants which need their weekly baths this month more than ever. Some may call for cutting back if they are getting leggy. Also check out the root systems to see if they are potbound. Continue to water forced bulbs until their tops turn yellow and then store them in pots until you can shift them outdoors.

Otherwise, continue all the precautions imposed by the season. Make sure your automatic ventilating system works, and check the location of the tropicals—a few extra minutes of cold air can harm them. As the days get longer, the larger-leafed plants will need more water, so it is advisable to observe them a bit more closely for signs of wilting or drying out.

Continue to be a good greenhouse keeper by forming the habit of picking dead blooms and foliage every day. Don't let debris pile up because the warmer days are going to stir up your old pest enemies. The aphids, mealy bugs and red spiders will reappear, and can cause heavy plant infestation, particularly if you've been careless.

If you've been lucky enough to get your hands on a pair of second-hand, but sound, storm doors, you'll find it's quite easy to put together an electric hotbed which should give you a really early start on spring. Make the frame to fit the storm doors which you'll use for covers, hinging them to the 12-inch-high boards. Set the frame on the bare (and frozen) ground in the full sun—the south side of the house near an electric outlet is recommended—and fill in with two inches of sand. Set the electric heating cable on the sand and cover with vermiculite. The cable comes with a regulating thermostat (set it at 60-65 degrees); a 24-foot unit costs about $15. Such a unit will pay for itself in a season or two by getting you off to early starts as well as prolonging the season and making it easy to maintain successive cropping.

March

How Soon Can We (Safely) Plant Outside?

... it is obvious that in point of weather an unbridled way-wardness prevails in our climate, and nothing can be done against it.

Yes, nothing can be done; it is the middle of March, and snow lies on the frozen ground. Lord, be merciful to the little flowers of the gardeners.

The Gardener's Year
Karel Capek

Vegetables, not "little flowers," are our concern at this critical time when "nothing can be done" because it is the "middle of March." However, we think *something can be done* and so we are putting together some guides which should help us all get our vegetable patches off to the fastest and best possible start. Consult and compare the guidelines when making your planting plans.

1) We have itemized the dates of the last-expected spring frosts by zone to give them the prominence they deserve.

2) We have grouped the more popular vegetables according to their cold and heat preferences so they can be quickly scanned and referred to.

3) We are including a truncated but working table that itemizes the earliest safe planting dates, plus the range of spring-planting dates in the open, *according to vegetable*. The given dates apply only to residents in Zones Two, Three, Four, and Five—frost dates extending from March 20 through May 10.

It's obvious that we all want to make the first planting of each crop as soon as it can be done safely. We're not only impatient to get started—we also would like to make second plantings later in the season. First, check your location on the zoned map inside the front cover, and commit firmly to memory the frost dates that apply to your garden.

Next comes our general but practical grouping of the more popular vegetables that most of us will plant, serve and preserve this year. Bear in mind—and this is where we differ with author Karel Capek—that many vegetables are so resistant to cold that they can be planted a month before the average date of the last freeze or about six weeks before the frost-free date. So, something can be done! According to USDA experts, the frost-free date is usually two to three weeks later in the spring than the average date of the last freeze, and falls on or near the date that the oak trees leaf out. And now, here are the more popular vegetables grouped according to the approximate times they can be planted and according to their relative requirements for cool and warm weather.

Bear in mind, while you're making your plans that most, if not all, of the cold-tolerant crops actually thrive better in cool weather than in hot. This means they should not be planted late in the spring in the southern parts of the country where hot summers prevail. *Therefore, the gardener should time his planting not only to escape the cold, but—with certain crops— also to escape the heat.* This should present no great problem. As most experienced gardeners know, vegetables that will not prosper when planted in late spring where the summers are hot, may be sown in late summer so they will do most of their growing in the cooler weather.

The closely detailed chart of last-frost dates plus the range of planting dates for our more common vegetables follows. Folks in Zones One and Seven will not benefit from the information presented in the chart, but the great majority of our

Early Planting Dates for Vegetables
March 20-May 10

Crop	Planting dates for localities with average last freeze on—		
	Mar. 20	Mar. 30	Apr. 10
Asparagus[1]	Feb. 1–Mar. 10	Feb. 15–Mar. 20	Mar. 10–Apr. 10
Beans, lima	Apr. 1–June 15	Apr. 15–June 20	Apr. 15–June 30
Beans, snap	Mar. 15–May 25	Apr. 1–June 1	Apr. 10–June 30
Beets	Feb. 15–May 15	Mar. 1–June 1	Mar. 10–June 1
Broccoli, sprouting[1]	Feb. 15–Mar. 15	Mar. 1–20	Mar. 15–Apr. 15
Brussels sprouts[1]	do	do	do
Cabbage[1]	Feb. 15–Mar. 20	Feb. 15–Mar. 10	Mar. 1–Apr. 1
Cabbage, Chinese	(2)	(2)	(2)
Carrots	Feb. 15–Mar. 20	Mar. 1–Apr. 10	Mar. 10–Apr. 20
Cauliflower[1]	Feb. 10–Mar. 10	Feb. 20–Mar. 20	Mar. 1–Mar. 20
Celery and celeriac	Mar. 1–Apr. 1	Mar. 15–Apr. 15	Apr. 1–Apr. 20
Chard	Feb. 20–May 15	Mar. 1–May 25	Mar. 15–June 15
Chervil and chives	Feb. 10–Mar. 10	Feb. 15–Mar. 15	Mar. 1–Apr. 1
Chicory, witloof	June 1–July 1	June 1–July 1	June 10–July 1
Collards[1]	Feb. 15–May 1	Mar. 1–June 1	Mar. 1–June 1
Corn salad	Jan. 1–Mar. 15	Jan. 15–Mar. 15	Feb. 1–Apr. 1
Corn, sweet	Mar. 15–May 1	Mar. 25–May 15	Apr. 10–June 1
Cress, upland	Feb. 20–Mar. 15	Mar. 1–Apr. 1	Mar. 10–Apr. 15
Cucumbers	Apr. 1–May 1	Apr. 10–May 15	Apr. 20–June 1
Dandelion	Feb. 10–Mar. 10	Feb. 20–Mar. 20	Mar. 1–Apr. 1
Eggplant[1]	Apr. 1–May 1	Apr. 15–May 15	May 1–June 1
Endive	Mar. 1–Apr. 1	Mar. 10–Apr. 10	Mar. 15–Apr. 15
Florence fennel	do	do	do
Garlic	Feb. 1–Mar. 1	Feb. 10–Mar. 10	Feb. 20–Mar. 20
Horseradish[1]		Mar. 1–Apr. 1	Mar. 10–Apr. 10
Kale	Feb. 20–Mar. 10	Mar. 1–20	Mar. 10–Apr. 1
Kohlrabi	do	Mar. 1–Apr. 1	Mar. 10–Apr. 10
Leeks	Feb. 1–Mar. 1	Feb. 15–Mar. 15	Mar. 1–Apr. 1
Lettuce, head[1]	Feb. 15–Mar. 10	Mar. 1–20	Mar. 10–Apr. 1
Lettuce, leaf	Feb. 1–Apr. 1	Feb. 15–Apr. 15	Mar. 15–May 15
Mustard	Feb. 20–Apr. 1	Mar. 1–Apr. 15	Mar. 10–Apr. 20
Okra	Apr. 1–June 15	Apr. 10–June 15	Apr. 20–June 15
Onions[1]	Feb. 10–Mar. 10	Feb. 15–Mar. 15	Mar. 1–Apr. 1
Onions, seed	do	Feb. 20–Mar. 15	do
Onions, sets	Feb. 1–Mar. 20	Feb. 15–Mar. 20	do
Parsley	Feb. 15–Mar. 15	Mar. 1–Apr. 1	Mar. 10–Apr. 10
Parsnips	do	do	do
Peas, garden	Feb. 1–Mar. 15	Feb. 10–Mar. 20	Feb. 20–Mar. 20
Peas, black-eye	Apr. 1–July 1	Apr. 15–July 1	May 1–July 1
Peppers[1]	Apr. 10–June 1	Apr. 15–June 1	May 1–June 1
Potatoes	Feb. 10–Mar. 15	Feb. 20–Mar. 20	Mar. 10–Apr. 1
Radishes	Jan. 20–May 1	Feb. 15–May 1	Mar. 1–May 1
Rhubarb[1]			Mar. 1–Apr. 1
Rutabagas	Jan. 15–Mar. 1	Feb. 1–Mar. 1	
Salsify	Feb. 15–Mar. 1	Mar. 1–15	Mar. 10–Apr. 15
Shallots	Feb. 1–Mar. 10	Feb. 15–Mar. 15	Mar. 1–Apr. 1
Sorrel	Feb. 10–Mar. 20	Feb. 20–Apr. 1	Mar. 1–Apr. 15
Soybeans	Apr. 10–June 30	Apr. 20–June 30	May 1–June 30
Spinach	Jan. 15–Mar. 15	Feb. 1–Mar. 20	Feb. 15–Apr. 1
Spinach, New Zealand	Apr. 1–May 15	Apr. 10–June 1	Apr. 20–June 1
Squash, summer	do	do	do
Sweet potatoes[1]	Apr. 10–June 1	Apr. 20–June 1	May 1–June 1
Tomatoes[1]	Apr. 1–May 20	Apr. 10–June 1	Apr. 20–June 1
Turnips	Feb. 10–Mar. 10	Feb. 20–Mar. 20	Mar. 1–Apr. 1

[1] Plants   [2] Planted in fall only

Earliest safe planting dates and range of spring-planting dates for vegetables

Crop	Planting dates for localities with average last freeze on—		
	Apr. 20	Apr. 30	May 10
Asparagus[1]	Mar. 15–Apr. 15.	Mar. 20–Apr. 15.	Apr. 10–Apr. 30.
Beans, lima	May 1–June 20	May 15–June 15.	May 25–June 15.
Beans, snap	Apr. 25–June 30.	May 10–June 30.	May 10–June 30.
Beets	Mar. 20–June 1.	Apr. 1–June 15	Apr. 15–June 15.
Broccoli, sprouting[1]	Mar. 25–Apr. 20.	Apr. 1–May 1	Apr. 15–June 1
Brussels sprouts[1]	do	do	do
Cabbage[1]	Mar. 10–Apr. 1.	Mar. 15–Apr. 10.	Apr. 1–May 15
Cabbage, Chinese	(2)	(2)	do
Carrots	Apr. 1–May 15	Apr. 10–June 1	Apr. 20–June 15.
Cauliflower[1]	Mar. 15–Apr. 20.	Apr. 10–May 10.	Apr. 15–May 15.
Celery and celeriac	Apr. 10–May 1	Apr. 15–May 1	Apr. 20–June 15.
Chard	Apr. 1–June 15	Apr. 15–June 15.	do
Chervil and chives	Mar. 10–Apr. 10.	Mar. 20–Apr. 20.	Apr. 1–May 1
Chicory, witloof	June 15–July 1.	June 15–July 1.	June 1–20
Collards[1]	Mar. 10–June 1	Apr. 1–June 1	Apr. 15–June 1
Corn salad	Feb. 15–Apr. 15.	Mar. 1–May 1	Apr. 1–June 1
Corn, sweet	Apr. 25–June 15.	May 10–June 15.	May 10–June 1
Cress, upland	Mar. 20–May 1.	Apr. 10–May 10.	Apr. 20–May 20.
Cucumbers	May 1–June 15...	May 15–June 15.	May 20–June 15.
Dandelion	Mar. 10–Apr. 10.	Mar. 20–Apr. 20.	Apr. 1–May 1
Eggplant[1]	May 10–June 1	May 15–June 10.	May 20–June 15.
Endive	Mar. 25–Apr. 15	Apr. 1–May 1	Apr. 15–May 15.
Florence fennel	do	do	do
Garlic	Mar. 10–Apr. 1	Mar. 15–Apr. 15.	Apr. 1–May 1
Horseradish[1]	Mar. 20–Apr. 20.	Apr. 1–30	Apr. 15–May 15.
Kale	Mar. 20–Apr. 10.	Apr. 1–20	Apr. 10–May 1
Kohlrabi	Mar. 20–May 1	Apr. 1–May 10	Apr. 10–May 15.
Leeks	Mar. 15–Apr. 15.	Apr. 1–May 1	Apr. 15–May 15.
Lettuce, head[1]	Mar. 20–Apr. 15.	do	do
Lettuce, leaf	Mar. 20–May 15	Apr. 1–June 1	Apr. 15–June 15.
Mustard	Mar. 20–May 1.	Apr. 1–May 10	Apr. 15–June 1
Okra	May 1–June 1	May 10–June 1	May 20–June 10
Onions[1]	Mar. 15–Apr. 10.	Apr. 1–May 1	Apr. 10–May 1
Onions, seed	Mar. 15–Apr. 1	Mar. 15–Apr. 15.	Apr. 1–May 1
Onions, sets	Mar. 10–Apr. 1	Mar. 10–Apr. 10.	Apr. 10–May 1
Parsley	Mar. 20–Apr. 20.	Apr. 1–May 1	Apr. 15–May 15.
Parsnips	do	do	do
Peas, garden	Mar. 10–Apr. 10.	Mar. 20–May 1	Apr. 1–May 15
Peas, black-eye	May 10–June 15.	May 15–June 1	
Peppers[1]	May 10–June 1	May 15–June 10.	May 20–June 10.
Potatoes	Mar. 15–Apr. 10.	Mar. 20–May 10.	Apr. 1–June 1
Radishes	Mar. 10–May 10.	do	do
Rhubarb[1]	Mar. 10–Apr. 10.	Mar. 20–Apr. 15.	Apr. 1–May 1
Rutabagas		May 1–June 1	May 1–June 1
Salsify	Mar. 20–May 1	Apr. 1–May 15	Apr. 15–June 1
Shallots	Mar. 15–Apr. 15.	Apr. 1–May 1	Apr. 10–May 1
Sorrel	Mar. 15–May 1	Apr. 1–May 15...	Apr. 15–June 1
Soybeans	May 10–June 20.	May 15–June 15.	May 25–June 10.
Spinach	Mar. 1–Apr. 15	Mar. 20–Apr. 20.	Apr. 1–June 15
Spinach, New Zealand	May 1–June 15	May 1–June 15	May 10–June 15.
Squash, summer	do	May 1–30	May 10–June 10.
Sweet potatoes[1]	May 10–June 10.	May 20–June 10.	
Tomatoes[1]	May 5–June 10	May 10–June 15.	May 15–June 10.
Turnips	Mar. 10–Apr. 1	Mar. 20–May 1	Apr. 1–June 1

[1] Plants [2] Planted in fall only

readers can base their planting calendars on the information given here.

And now, it remains only to pray for clement weather; soft rains when you need them, benevolent sunshine and gentle nights when, if you listen, you can hear the earth breathe.

The Vegetable Garden

WIRE CAGE TO HOLD LEAVES

2' DEEP

MULCH 6-8"

SHREDDED LEAVES

PULL BACK MULCH TO GATHER POTATOES AS NEEDED.

Gardeners from Zone Four northward can cut asparagus one to two weeks sooner by leaving half the bed unmulched—the soil will heat up faster that way—while doing an otherwise thorough job of renovation. As soon as the weather permits, use a rotary mower or shredder to shred the old plants you left standing over the winter. Spread this aggregate and a layer of compost or rotted manure (if you neglected to do so last fall) over the other half of the bed. Then mulch this portion heavily with cocoa bean shells or finely-ground corncobs.

Zone Two growers can plant spinach and peas outdoors as soon as the soil is open, although in Pennsylvania, we have planted our peas as early as January in fall-prepared soils. We wait for a melt and thaw and drop the seed into a shallow furrow which we close by hand. We frequently get quite early peas in a generous season which also gives us a head start with our corn plantings.

Gardeners in the broad-belt of Zone Three can plant peas, spinach and onion sets outdoors by the middle of the month —the weather permitting. Inside, on the windowsill or on the porch, you should start tomatoes, peppers, eggplant and Malabar spinach. Work with individual peat pots, three or four seeds to the container, and thin to one plant later.

Move them to your hotbed as soon as possible—as soon as they have germinated and are growing. Set them in a warmer corner where they are protected from any straying spring breezes and be prepared to blanket well at night.

Onions, lettuce, carrots, radishes and turnips may be planted in the Zone Three central states as soon as the maples bloom. Cover crops should be turned under as soon as the ground can be worked, and rows prepared for spinach, garlic and corn salad.

All hardy vegetables should be planted as soon as possible in Zone Four. Included are beets, carrots, chard, chives, leeks, lettuce, mustard, onions, parsley, potatoes, salsify, plus members of the cabbage family—broccoli, Brussels sprouts, cauliflower, kale, turnips. With relenting weather, most of these may also be planted in Zone Three just before the end of the month.

Allow garlic and a few multiplier onions to make tops as they mature so you will have some sets for fall planting. The newly-planted sets should give you a better crop than multipliers left in the ground year after year.

Bush and lima beans may be planted this month in Zones Six and Seven, and other tender vegetables and melons may now also be set out safely. In Zone Five, bush beans, tomatoes, squash, corn and melons may be seeded outdoors after St. Patrick's Day; but limas and eggplant should be delayed in planting until next month.

Seed potatoes should sit on a bright but not sunny windowsill, and left to sprout. The smaller, egg-size spuds should give the best yield; many readers report that cutting the potatoes for planting seems to rob them of vitality. We like to plant ours about six to eight inches down in a two-feet-deep leaf bed held intact over the winter in a light wire enclosure. The spuds we get are sweet, much more tender than those grown in soil and cooked whole in their thin jackets, go very well in soups and stews.

Strawberry beds in Zone Three and southward should be uncovered when new green shoots appear. The plants should be thinned to stand nine or more inches apart in matted rows. If the beds have been free of disease, the lifted plants may be used to start new rows.

Don't rush the season with the strawberry beds. Be thrifty when removing the straw mulch as the new pale leaves make their appearance. Hold it handy in reserve—you may need it later should a sudden, late frost develop. The plants should be thinned to at least nine inches, with the woodier ones removed.

If you take young plants, use them to start rows. Do not give either young or bearing plants fertilizer, but rather delay feeding until after the harvest. Too much early spring fertilizer gives softer berries which are more susceptible to fungus. When you start new rows, try to situate them where no strawberries have been grown for the last six or even more years.

As the old plantings of root parsley, shallots, multiplier onions and garlic begin to make tops, thin them to clear the bed of next year's seedlings. Young shallots can be used like green onions while the multipliers will produce better plants if the top bulbs are removed and replanted in the fall. Before they begin to make growth dig and store in the refrigerator any carrots from the winter crop that are still in the ground.

It's time to plant soybeans, okra and canteloupe in the warmest sea-level areas of the Southwest, with peanuts going in later in the month. You can start now to set out onion and garlic sets, horseradish and asparagus roots, also the cabbage family, if you live no higher than Tombstone, and sow seed for peas, radishes, turnips, rutabaga, leeks, lettuce, kale, endive and chard. But wait until the end of the month to plant your potatoes.

As soon as leaves begin to appear on trees in the Pacific Coast area, hardy vegetables may be sown. Sweet peas and larkspur should go in as soon as possible in the gardens west of the Cascades, and peas and spinach may already have been sown. The late plantings should include beets, carrots, potatoes, lettuce, onions, garlic, chard, cabbages and turnips. Legumes will profit from an inoculation with nitrogen-fixing bacteria if no legumes were previously grown in their site.

Don't waste the inoculant on treated seeds—the poison on them will probably kill the bacteria.

Seeds should now be planted indoors in individual pots for the earliest sweet corn. When the nights turn warm, plant the seeds outdoors in the garden in clusters of three. Work with early-season varieties that mature within 65 days. Among these are: Early Golden Giant and Early Sunglow, both 63 days; Golden Midget and Spancross Hybrid, both 65 days; Golden Sunshine, 68 days.

The Ornamental Garden

As the month wanes and grows more lamblike, residents in Zones Two and Three can loosen the mulch in their flower borders without removing it. The wind screens should be kept around the ornamental evergreens until the March winds grow really gentle. If snow has been light most of the winter, it's a good idea to give these plants some water as soon as the soil thaws.

It's a bit early but worth mentioning—spring's first grass clippings are richer in nitrogen than those you will cut later in the season. So, as you clean up the lawn and start mowing, save all the first month's clippings for mulching your lettuce asparagus, early beets, cabbage and celery, all of which are big nitrogen feeders.

Actually, lawns in all areas need attention this month. Bermudagrass or St. Augustinegrass can be sprigged or plugged now from Zone Four south, while low spots should be repaired from Zone Three north as soon as the ground is open. On old lawns, spread one-half inch of screened compost mixed with bone meal. Test the soil before spreading limestone. Less of it is needed than is generally thought to keep the lawn pH at the ideal 6.0 to 7.0.

One-inch turf is permitted this time—three inches later—so

trim very closely and rake to remove all mat clippings. Aerate thoroughly—a fork will do the job—if you find no trace of earthworm castings under the mat. Spread the compost with a rake or stiff brush, working it into the aeration holes.

Follow the snow thaw north as closely as possible with plantings of larkspur and sweet peas. The hardy annuals can now be planted in Zone Four, the semi-hardy in Zone Five, and everything including the tenderest may be planted in Zones Six and Seven.

Succession plantings of gladioli may be started now by planting a new lot of corns in the cutting garden every ten days.

Central staters should spray their broad-leaved evergreens at this time with a weak oil-emulsion spray before they start their spring growth. The spray should be only half as strong as that used on deciduous trees.

In the central states, biennials can be transplanted to the borders when they have hardened off in the cold frames. Those that may be set out now include forget-me-not, foxglove, English daisies, sweet william, pansies, biennial campanulas and wallflowers. The empty spaces left in the cold frames may be filled with seedling annuals which should now be ready for transplanting.

Summer- and fall-flowering perennials should be divided and transplanted now, but the spring-blooming varieties should not be disturbed until they are finished flowering. Be careful not to smother their delicate crowns while spreading bone meal or well-rotted manure around such big feeders as bee balm, bleeding heart, delphiniums, peonies and Oriental poppies.

Easterners south of the Bluegrass Line dig up and divide the overgrown masses of summer- and fall-blooming perennials before they make any more growth. Take up the clumps separately, wash the excess soil off their roots and divide with a clean, sharp knife. Fill the vacated holes with as much compost as you can spare, plus rock phosphate, and dig the same mixture into the new planting holes.

Annuals may be sown in the upper South as soon as the trees begin to leaf out. Further south, annuals may be kept blooming by picking the old blossoms promptly, and giving the plants booster shots of liquid manure.

Keep planting French and African marigolds throughout the garden and in the vegetable patch. According to the Connecticut Experimental Station, they secrete a substance that knocks nematodes out of the soil. Many southern gardens have been cleared of eelworms when this practice is followed. But be sure to plant the smelly varieties—the deodorized ones are not rated effective.

Gardeners in Zones Two and Three should loosen but not remove the mulch in the bulb and perennial borders. Soggy leaves can be pulled away from the crown of delphiniums, foxglove and primroses while last year's winter-hilled shoots are removed from the plumbago, and the artemisia are cut back. As soon as they appear, whiten the soil around the spring-flowering bulbs with bone meal and stir in lightly.

Seeds of annual flowers may be planted in beds and borders further south while perennial seeds may be sown in the cold frame. Give the spring-flowering shrubs their annual pruning as soon as they are finished blooming. Also prune the summer- and fall-flowering shrubs but only to shape them. Be careful to delay the more serious trimming and paring until after they are done blooming.

Roses in the Southwest should be uncovered and pruned now. Remove the old mulch to the compost pile, and allow the soil two to three weeks to bake thoroughly before applying a fresh summer mulch of rotted manure. Zone Five residents are also safe in uncovering tender roses at this time, but frost may still be a threat in Zone Four until the end of the month. If you want exhibition blooms, prune the bushes vigorously after uncovering them.

In the Southwest, fuchsias may be set out in the warm areas in well-prepared beds that have been enriched with leaf mold. Further north, along the Pacific Coast, they should be pruned with the side shoots cut back to within a few inches of the stems—no more than three or four in number—to achieve bushy growth. Tree-form plants should be pruned to a single stem, and the tips of the top branches pinched back.

Roses should also be pruned this month in the Coastal area while their manure-straw mulch is renewed. Again, grass clippings from the first nitrogen-rich mowings make an excellent mulch.

The Orchard and Bush Fruits

1. REMOVE MULCH

It's planting time now up in Zone Three for deciduous trees, and close to finishing time for Zone Four and Five homesteaders. There's still time to order trees in the "up-north" areas, but it's running out, and you probably will have to work with local nurserymen. If this applies to you, console yourself with the knowledge that trees planted in your county or area should grow better there and suffer less transplanting shock.

If you are ordering through the mail, make sure the varieties you choose are hardy for your section—northern nurseries sometimes order their stock from southern growers. If in doubt, check with your local ag station for recommended varieties.

Grafting should be done as soon as the buds begin to swell. If you have self-infertile trees, try grafting onto them scions of varieties which are suitable for cross-pollination. Spread pulverized rock fertilizers under the orchard trees and berry bushes, working the additives into the top layer of soil before applying the summer mulch. Also give them the annual nitrogen-rich feeding of organic fertilizers, if it hasn't been done.

2 SPREAD ORGANIC FERTILIZERS

3. COVER GROUND WITH ROCKS BEFORE REPLACING MULCH

After removing mulch from under the fruit trees, spread rock fertilizers plus a nitrogen-rich substance like compost, blood meal or cottonseed meal. Toss a sizeable collection of rocks and stones under the trees before spreading the new mulch—they will shelter worms that work near the surface, keeping the soil cool enough for them far into the summer when most worms dig down far below the surface. The rocks also conserve soil moisture that might evaporate by condensing it on their undersides, making it available in the root area.

Bramble fruits should be cut back and tied this month. Blackberries and most of the others should be held to five feet at the most. The few exceptions include Snyder blackberries, 36 inches, with laterals held to seven to ten buds; Lawton should be pruned to two-thirds its original length with the laterals cut one half. Bailey can grow six feet tall; the red raspberries four feet, with only eight to 12 canes to the plant; all blackberry canes less than one-half inch at the base should be cut out, leaving no more than four to six canes per plant, with laterals no more than six to eight inches long.

Up in Zones Two and Three, apple growers have their last chance this month to insure a pest-free crop for 1972 by cleaning up their trees. Using a hoe, scrape off all the loose bark. It's advisable to spread a tarpaulin under the tree first, so you catch all the scrapings to which codling moth cocoons stick.

Follow this by wrapping a loose band of burlap around the trunk to lure summer larvae to where you will be able to get at them conveniently and destroy them. Spray the trees with dormant oil against scale and mites, and place a sticky band around the trunk to catch female cankerworms when they crawl up to lay their eggs in the fruit. Finally, order trichogramma eggs so they will hatch in the trees when the codling moths lay their eggs in your area. Your county agent will be glad to give you the local egg-laying timetables.

Further south, fruit trees and woody ornamentals should be fed and pruned. While pruning of figs may be completed at this time, drastic cutting back of winterkill on citrus fruits should be deferred until mid-summer. Only small dead twigs and diseased growth should be removed now. Root cuttings of bramble fruits may be set out at this time. To discourage unwanted sucker growth, cultivate paths between rows of established bushes.

Zone Three central staters should prune and fertilize fruit and nut trees, grapevines and bush fruits at this time. Trees vulnerable to scale should be sprayed with a dormant oil before the buds open.

You've already got too much to do, and not enough time to do it in, but try to take advantage of every day the soil is workable to prepare holes for the trees and shrubs you order for spring delivery. You most surely will need the old-fashioned mattock to get started, but we have found that the vertically-applied posthole digger is fine for enlarging the hole while making its sides straight and, incidentally, getting more soil out of the excavation. Try it for finishing—seems to work faster and better.

Should the plants arrive before you are ready for them, store them outside in the shade. If you've made a trench or have one handy—fine. Otherwise cover the roots with damp cloths and burlap, and keep the roots moist at all times. Be sure to keep everything away from the direct rays of the sun, or steady winds. All deciduous materials should be safely in the ground before leafing out; they will stand the summer better for being planted as soon as possible.

Avocado trees may be planted in the warmest sections of the Southwest. The young trees require rich soil, good drainage, and a continual mulch of rich compost. The sensitive young trees should be protected for the first year from the sun, and for three years from even light, brief frosts.

Homesteaders in the Southwest who find that their alkali soil makes it hard to grow small fruits might try this treatment which reportedly has worked for other gardeners in the area. Dig in as much sharp builders' sand, steer manure and leaf mold as you can. Then mulch the plants—raspberries, peaches, strawberries, or whatever—with grass clippings or alfalfa hay.

Apricots and other woody deciduous trees and shrubs should be planted now on the West Coast, and before the middle of the month in the southern areas, and before the first week in April further north. Where late frosts can be expected, plant the apricots where they will have a northern exposure, so flowering will be delayed in the spring. It's also time now to spread compost, tankage, manure and bone meal around the woody ornamentals, fruit trees and vines.

On the West Coast, winter-killed growth should be pruned back once it is certain that it will not revive. Compost, manures and rock fertilizers should be spread around fruit trees, grapevines, bush fruits and all woody ornamentals. The bramble fruits such as blackberries and boysenberries, should be tied and pruned back. Bush varieties that were pinched back last summer should have their laterals cut back half their length. All raspberry canes should be trimmed one-third.

In the colder areas where, last summer, the trailing varieties could not be pruned and tied, they should be cut now and trained to their supports. On all varieties, allow no more than ten canes to develop on the largest plants, and only six on the younger or smaller ones. All pruning should be completed before the buds begin to swell and expand.

Under Glass

PLANT 3. — THIN TO 1.

This is the month, up North, for winter's worst storms to strike, although warm afternoons and even nights may be the rule south of the Bluegrass Line. So you will do well to keep the more sensitive plants away from the exposed areas while increasing daytime ventilation. If there is full sun and little or no wind, the roof ventilators may be opened to their widest. And, if the outside temperature pushes past 50 degrees, you can open the side ventilators and doors.

The extra care should help you control the aphids, mealy bugs, red spiders and fungi. In addition to ventilating judiciously as indicated, spray the plants with a stream of water every sunny morning. Also, keep the lids open on the cold frame to harden off the plants, and be sure to give them more water and food as the days lengthen.

Do the same for the windowsill plants, moving the seedlings to the cold frame but, again, taking care at night to protect the frames against those unpredictable cold snaps.

It's time to put the hotbeds and cold frames into condition, assuming you haven't already done so. Check their ventilation carefully, especially on the sunny and promising days. The covers should be closed without fail at night, but kept open during the day according to the intensity and amount of sun-light—from the merest slit or crack to a good-sized opening.

Meanwhile the seeds should be sown in equal parts of compost and sand in flats and pots. If the seedlings are to be transplanted, prepare the site with equal parts of soil, sand and compost or well-rotted manure.

You can start your first sowings of zucchini and Swiss chard now in individual pots in the greenhouse or on a warm side porch that gets plenty of sun. You can follow up this early start later in the garden after the soil warms up.

Broccoli, eggplant, celery, tomatoes and still more lettuce can be started now in flats. The tenderer vegetables—this includes snap beans, cucumbers, okra, New Zealand spinach, soybeans, squash, corn, limas, peppers and sweet potatoes—should be kept inside until the nights are safely warm; they will suffer less transplanting shock.

This same problem applies if your greenhouse is prin-cipally a kitchen windowsill. Be sure to protect the tender seedlings from the glass on the cold March nights. One hard chill may or may not kill the plants, but they can be set back so badly that they will be slow in recovering and ultimately in producing. Again, tomatoes, peppers and eggplant are in this sensitive group.

Keep the seedlings of the more tender vegetables—tomatoes, peppers, and eggplant—growing rapidly. Give them a 75-degree day temperature, 65 degrees at night, and feed them every other week with manure water or fish fertilizer.

Transfer the seedlings you have been growing at the kitchen window to the outdoor cold frame—if you think they can stand it. The plants will be less leggy if grown and brought along outdoors than if they reach garden size at the window.

Those that should be able to handle the transition—given a little benevolent weather—include broccoli, cabbage, lettuce, onions, peas, potatoes, spinach, turnips, beets, carrots, chard, parsnips and radishes. But keep an old blanket or two, or a couple of straw-filled burlap bags handy, just in case.

Here's a gamble that doesn't cost much and may win you some admiration in the neighborhood. If you want to try for the earliest corn around, prepare a dozen or more five-inch pots with three seeds each. Later, when they reach the three-inch mark, thin them to one seedling to the pot. Remember that corn thrives on heat when you give the pots a place. Work with some 63- to 65-day varieties, and don't be too disappointed when the seeds you sow out later in the planting row come on strong and catch up to your pampered pets. Recommended 63- to 66-day varieties are Early Sunglow, Spancross, Earliking and Early Golden Giant.

Late January or early February chrysanthemum cuttings should be potted now for late-spring bloom. Give them extra light from 5 to 10 p.m. for a week, then shade from 5 p.m. to 8 a.m. for the next three weeks. Pinch once to stimulate side branching.

The hardy mums that have been stored in the cold frames should now be brought indoors. Old growth should be cut back to promote new which will be used for cuttings in April and May. Seedlings of annual plants, grown from January seeding, should be set on benches, spaced at six-inch intervals in rows that are eight inches apart.

Although episcia may be propagated any time, March seems to be the best month for getting started. Terminal stem cuttings, leaf cuttings or runners will root in any media—we like rich potting soil—if given 65-degree bottom heat. Shift to three-inch pots or larger when ready. Episcia may also be grown from seeds planted at this time. Varieties include E. chontalensis; E. cupreata; E. dianthiflora; E. viridifolia.

From now on plants under glass will need more water and food because the longer days mean more growing time for them. This situation applies equally to window plants, also those in the greenhouse, the hotbed or cold frame. It's also not too early now to start dividing and repotting house plants. After repotting, keep them shaded and well-watered for one week before returning them to their windows.

Perennials that may be sown now under glass for later transplanting to the borders include coral bell, delphinium, foxglove, sweet william, gaillardia, hollyhocks, phlox, pyrethrum and achillea. Annuals that may be sown for indoor bloom include snapdragons, stocks, mimosa and sweet peas.

After St. Patrick's Day, start to harden off early cabbages, seven-week stocks and nemesia for planting out in April.

Hold back the last of your potted forced bulbs. They will brighten your window boxes on Easter morning.

It will pay you to visit your nearest spring garden show where you should be able to observe many new and attractive greenhouse practices. The new flower and vegetable varieties should stimulate you to new experiments on your own, while the various extension service booths may help you solve some of the problems that have been bothering you all winter.

April
April Is a Green Month

Life's sweetest joys are hidden
In unsubstantial things;
An April rain, a fragrance....

The Treetop Road
May Riley

April is a cheerful month, a green month in which we are encouraged to display our collective folk wisdom in the preparation and early cultivation of our gardens. Among the factors responsible for this rush of optimistic activity is the fact that April is also a rainy month which seems to promise well for the rest of the year.

We've been checking into this matter of rainfall, climate and crops, and since we always look forward to a highly productive year, this is the place and time to share our findings.

At one time it was thought that the amount of rainfall in an area was directly dependent upon the amount of local soil moisture evaporation. In other words, more evaporation of water from the soil would bring about more rain in an area.

53

This led to a very interesting, if painful, experiment that was conducted over a 10-year period in the Great Plains States.

The farmers were induced to plant trees by the passage of legislation in Congress—the Timber Culture Act of 1873. For a while all went well. Farmers planted trees steadily, and from 1875 to 1886 "abundant rainfall occurred in the Great Plains." The theory was strongly—but erroneously—advanced that "a spread in cultivation had changed the hydrolic balance in favor of increased rainfall." It was felt that the soil acted like a huge sponge after it was broken, absorbing and storing moisture, so that as cultivation was extended, more and more rainfall would be conserved, and "increased rainfall would result from the increased evaporation."

The myth that a human agency—plus trees—was responsible for the increased rainfall in the Plains was brusquely shattered by the subsequent period of drought. Failure to recognize that the atmosphere doesn't stand still over one area, and that moisture can be carried great distances was thus blamed for the overextension of agriculture in that part of the country.

Today, it is hard to refrain from wondering what might have happened if the farmers had practiced mulching during that benevolent 10-year period. Instead, researchers report, "commercial interests found it to their advantage to publicize this hypothesis (more evaporation means more rain) which became a factor in the great exploitation of dry-land farms."

Rainfall is rather scanty in the Great Plains which extend in a pretty straight north-south line from Texas up to Montana and the Dakotas. It averages less than 20 inches annually except in the warmer southern areas, and only slightly more than 10 inches in the north. It can vary greatly from a bad year to a good, ranging from less than 10 inches to more than 30.

Rain in the eastern part of the country is caused by the interaction of arctic air with semi-tropical masses from the south. The northern climate is described as "polar continental" by the experts, while its southern counterpart is known as "tropical maritime." The path followed by warm southern flow of air curves across the Gulf of Mexico, up the Mississippi, and then eastward toward the Atlantic. During this trip it is forced upward by the arctic masses, is cooled in the process, and so falls to the earth as rain.

Occasionally masses of very moist tropical air invade the Plains States, where they collide with dry polar air with such force that "violent rainstorms and heavy precipitation occur." When this happens it can bring as much as one-third of the average annual supply in just one day, or even one-fifth of the annual supply in one hour. On the other hand, 120 days can pass in this area without a single drop of rain.

Quantity does not tell the whole story. Slope and soil texture determine how much rain the ground can hold *and how much good it will ultimately do.* In some areas, trees grow on the north slope and grasses on the south. Or grasses can grow on the north slope and desert shrubs on the south. Finally, when the terrain and climate are severe, desert shrubs grow on the north slope while the south is bare of vegetation.

But, averaging north and south slopes, the friable and the crusted soils, the experts find that runoff amounts to 30 percent of the annual precipitation, while evaporation is about 70 percent. No need to point out to the organic gardener how mulching can affect these figures in his own back yard! We all know that mulched soil will hold more moisture simply by cutting down on runoff and evaporation.

Average Rainfall and Melted Snow Water

(in inches)

	Lon-don	Paris	Ber-lin	Rome	Mos-cow	To-kyo	Bom-bay	New York	Cape-town	Syd-ney
Jan.	1.9	1.5	1.9	3.6	1.6	2.3	0.1	3.5	0.7	3.9
Feb.	1.6	1.2	1.3	2.7	1.4	3.0	0.1	3.1	0.6	3.2
March . . .	1.6	1.6	1.5	3.1	1.4	4.3	0.0	3.6	0.8	4.4
April . . .	1.6	1.7	1.6	3.1	1.4	5.3	0.0	3.2	1.9	5.6
May	1.8	2.1	1.9	2.4	1.9	5.9	0.6	3.5	3.7	5.0
June	2.0	2.3	2.3	1.8	2.5	6.8	19.8	3.7	4.4	3.7
July	2.2	2.2	3.2	0.8	3.1	5.6	23.9	4.2	3.6	4.9
Aug.	2.2	2.2	2.2	1.0	2.8	7.1	14.1	4.3	3.3	2.4
Sept. . . .	1.9	2.0	1.9	3.0	2.4	10.1	10.6	3.7	2.3	2.8
Oct.	2.6	2.3	1.7	5.3	2.5	7.9	2.1	3.0	1.6	2.8
Nov.	2.3	1.8	1.7	4.5	1.8	3.5	0.5	3.1	1.0	2.5
Dec.	2.3	1.7	1.9	4.1	1.6	2.2	0.1	3.1	0.8	3.6
Year	24.0	22.6	23.1	35.4	24.4	64.0	71.9	42.0	24.7	44.8
Days of rain .	164	173	171	106	184	148	75	126	97	143
Days of snow .	13	12	32	2	91	16	0	16	0	0

Actually, annual precipitation varies enormously over the earth, ranging from less than one inch to more than 900—although the *Encyclopedia Britannica* lists Mt. Waialeale in Hawaii as the "wettest known point with a 20-year average of 460 inches, considerably ahead of second-place Cherrapunji in India with 426 inches." The difference—34 inches per year—would satisfy many of us if it were allotted to just our area.

We append here a chart showing the annual rainfall and melted snow waters for 10 principal cities. It's interesting to note that London, Paris, Berlin and Moscow—all lying more or less in the same degree of latitude—have the same amount of rainfall annually, 23-24 inches.

No matter where you live, one practice you'll benefit from most is mulching. Adjust yours to the season, sunlight and rain—but mulch. Use whatever is handy and abundant—but mulch. Nobody really knows whether this spring is going to be wet or dry.

But—wet or dry—keep the mulch handy and ready.

The Vegetable Garden

LEAVE OPEN FOR VENTILATION

1. TIE STURDY TWINE AROUND BOTTOM OF JUG. DAUB TWINE WITH GASOLINE.
2. SET AFIRE.
3. WHEN FLAMES DIE, DIP INTO PAN OF ICE WATER... BOTTOM BREAKS OFF NEATLY.
4. PLACE OVER TRANSPLANTS OR SEEDS IN THE GARDEN.

This is the heavy vegetable-planting month in all sections except those pressing the Canadian border and the Mexican Gulf. The peas should be in the ground by now, assuming you advance-prepared the soil in the fall. At their first opportunity, Zone One and Two gardeners should plant seeds of beets, carrots, lettuce, onions, spinach, turnips and radishes.

If their soil is workable, Zone Two gardeners already have planted their peas. During a mid-winter thaw in eastern Pennsylvania we quite frequently plant ours in soil that had been advance-prepared. Just scratch a shallow furrow, drop the inoculated peas in, and then pat over them. Always plant early peas that way. Next on the list are onions, both seed and set, lettuce, carrots, beets, turnips for greens, radishes and cabbage.

Seed potatoes may be started now in the earth or in beds of shredded leaves and then covered with more leaves and straw. They should be sprouted before planting, and each egg-sized cutting should have one good, strong sprout.

In Zone Three, all hardy vegetables should be in, and by the end of the month the first sowings of string beans, corn and squash will be made. Tomato plants can also be set out before the end of the month, but stand ready to give them good protection which is almost certain to be needed—at least once. Bottomless glass jugs—it's a knack doing it with a glass cutter, a bit of string and gasoline—will collect the sun's warmth and hold it through most nights. Or you can invest in the new styrofoam hotcaps which will do even better and are reputed to last for years in the garden.

If the spring is warm and sunny and the soil responds, Zone Three gardeners may also plant their cantaloupes and watermelons near the end of the month. Set them in compost-enriched hills along an edge of the garden where they will have room to run towards the sun.

Tomatoes may be planted now in the sandy-loam sections of the upper South, provided you keep a watchful eye out for sudden frosts. It will not be safe in the clay-loam piedmont regions to plant tomatoes or any other tender vegetables outside until the end of the month. Be sure to protect the new transplants from cutworms with paper collars—bottomless tin cans are even better.

In the far South, second plantings of bush and pole beans can go in this month, plus collard, cantaloupes, okra, pumpkins, spinach, mustard and watermelons. Roselle started now, will make a pleasant annual hedge and later provide a cranberry-flavored jelly.

Both bush and pole beans may be set out after the danger of frost has passed. Plant peanuts when the soil is a little warmer, and later in the month set out eggplant, okra, peppers sweet potatoes and lima beans. Sometime between the tomatoes and eggplant, plant squash, melons and cucumbers.

As soon as the weather settles down in the central states, the main corn crop that will go in the freezer, should be planted. Finish planting out the cool-weather vegetables, and begin to harden off the tomatoes and peppers. While, with protection, these may be planted by the middle of the month in more favored areas, the sunflowers, watermelons and cantaloupes can be planted two weeks before the last expected frost.

But all three will need hot exposure and plenty of compost, manure and rock fertilizers. Be shrewd about your mulching; delay it as long as you safely can in order to warm the soil as deeply as possible and yet not lose too much moisture.

Gardens in the southwest region should be treated individually according to altitude. By now they should be almost entirely planted from sea level up to 1,000 feet. At 3,500 feet the last of the hardy vegetables should be coming up, and many tender plants may now be sown.

Tomatoes, eggplant, peppers and okra can be set out in the middle of the month, given moderate night protection, and limas can go into the ground just before the month ends. At about 5,000 feet, gardeners are about ready now to plant the first hardy crops, but should not think about tender plantings this month. Salad greens can now be set out in the lower areas under a lath house. Compost piles should not be neglected at this time. They should be kept moist and built up with garden weeds, grass clippings, kitchen garbage, rock fertilizers and any manure that is too fresh for the garden.

In the hot Southwest, mulch is possibly more important than in any other area. Composting, if you water conscientiously, should be somewhat easier here than elsewhere, so there should be plenty of material in which to get your plants well-started before the really hot weather sets in. Build it up with all available crop residues, including grass clippings—the first are richest in nitrogen, manure that is too hot for the garden, rock fertilizers and kitchen wastes. Again, keep the heap moist, and protect it from the hottest sun and drying winds.

It's time to start the summer's salad greens under shade and in a cold frame from which you have removed the glass.

Asparagus cutting should be just starting now in parts of Zone Two and throughout Zone Three. It should be in full swing in Zones Four and Five, and coming to a stop further south in Zones Six and Seven. Weeding your asparagus bed as you pick through it each day is the best way to keep it in first-class condition. It should be fairly clear of weeds by the end of the cutting season, and a good mulch will be all that it needs until fall.

Have you any ducks or chickens? They'll be interested in the asparagus beetle—a metallic blue-black insect, with a squarish, yellowish pattern at the edges of his dark wings. Her eggs appear as blackish specks on the asparagus spears. If you find either—specks or beetles—turn your ducks or chickens into the patch at the end of the harvest. They'll take care of the beetles.

Thin the strawberries to about nine inches after they have been uncovered. When thinning, save the young, vigorous growth while discarding those whose bases seem woody. Follow the same procedure when selecting plants for the new rows from the thinnings—work with the younger plants. Keep cover material handy when cold nights threaten the tender young blooms and watch out for the late frosts.

All vegetables may be set out safely now along the southern end of the Pacific Coast. But wait a few weeks more before starting the hot-weather crops in the central area. Only the cool-weather vegetables should be planted now in the northern zones. This includes white potatoes, spinach, beets, carrots, turnips, onions, radishes, cabbage, lettuce and carrots. Asparagus roots can also be planted, providing the soil is workable to a depth of 18 to 24 inches. Gardeners in Zones Six and Seven can use their lath houses for lettuce, and further north, in Zones Four and Five, globe artichoke suckers should be transplanted.

The Ornamental Garden

CHRYSANTHEMUMS

WATER WELL & MULCH.

DISCARD WOODY CENTER

HUSKY OUTER SHOOTS BEST FOR RESETTING IN ENRICHED SOIL.

12~15"

Most lilies will appreciate a dusting of wood ashes now. Exceptions to the rule include L. amabile, L. auratum, L. formosum, L. hansoni, L. pumilum, L. superbum and L. tigrinum. If frost should threaten after the Madonna lilies are up, cover them with hotcaps or baskets or they may be unable to bloom.

Dahlia tubers may be brought out into a warm, lit place for sprouting before being planted out. After the young shoots make their appearance, separate the tubers to leave at least one vital shoot on each division, and then plant in a rich, well-dug bed.

Gladiolus bulbs may be planted now in Zones Three and Four to obtain the earliest possible bloom. For a longer season, follow the first plantings with successive ones every two weeks until June. You may now also plant alyssum, bachelor's button, balsam, calendula, nigella and poppies. But wait until the soil is warmer before setting out dahlias, nasturtiums, zinnias, tuberosas and the other more tender flowers and bulbs.

Check the iris to make sure there are no borers in the tubers. Where the leaves are not as plump as they should be and appear limp, look for hollow tubers and track down the fat, grub-like borers that can kill off your entire planting if not caught in time.

Aerate lawns this month in Zones Three through Five. Use a conventional garden fork for small places while aerating a larger area by running discs over it set four inches apart and three inches deep. Fill the holes and crevices with sieved compost.

In all sections, use early grass clippings for mulch because they are very rich in nitrogen at this time. While you're about it, whiten the soil around spring-flowering bulbs with bone meal, and sprinkle wood ashes around the delphiniums, grapes and fruit trees. You don't have to dig the ashes or meal under; the next spring rain will do the job for you.

Further south, the spring-flowering shrubs should be pruned as soon as they are through blooming while the fall-blooming perennials should be divided and replanted. Seeds can be sowed now for balsam, cosmos, four o'clocks, marigolds, petunias, portulaca and torenia. Plant out summer-flowering bulbs, cannas, caladiums, agave, yucca, clerodendron and pampasgrass. Give all woody ornamentals their annual feeding of nitrogen-rich fertilizers.

PINCH BACK SHOOTS AT 6 IN. – THEN EVERY MONTH 'TILL AUGUST.

In all areas where chrysanthemum growth has started, lift and divide the old plants now. Get rid of the woody central portions and place the rooted young shoots 12 to 15 inches apart in a generously enriched bed. Water them well and mulch. They should need no further care until the shoots are six inches tall and ready for the first pinching-back. For bushy plants full of flowers, continue to pinch back new growth until the first ten days of August.

Spread compost over the perennial borders, working it in carefully around plants such as delphiniums whose crowns should not be smothered. After the last hard freeze is safely past, transfer the hardy annual seedlings from the cold frame to the border. Roses can be pruned now in Zone Three. Dig in rotted manure around them, and then let the soil warm up in the sun for several weeks before applying mulch.

Central staters in the broad Zone Three belt will do much to revive their rock gardens by spreading a fresh layer of the finest gravel for mulch. Make sure that the foliage of such Alpine beauties as the encrusted saxifrages is well insulated from soil moisture by liberal amounts of stone chips. Webby specimens like Sempervivum arachnoidem should be protected from birds in search of nesting material by a temporary cover of wire mesh.

Planting of annuals further south should be completed by now. Divide and reset the summer- and fall-blooming perennials, also the cannas, glads and caladium bulbs. Mulch the soil around the lilies, and keep them well-watered while they make their growth.

Before the hot weather sets in, mulch the magnolias well, using manure if the plants have not been fed in the last three years. New plants can be propagated by pegging down a branch and covering the pegged portion with soil while leaving the tip exposed. In two years you should have a new plant.

Southwest residents should get ready now to mulch as heavily as possible to save water against a dry summer. While ground corncobs reinforced with compost are excellent for shrubs, something finer in texture will dress up the flower beds more prettily. Try sawdust, buckwheat hulls, cocoa bean shells or peat moss mixed with dried coffee shells or with dried coffee grounds. Only the native cactus can be permitted to go into the hot summer without a cover of mulch.

Azaleas should be mulched now in the Southwest with acid evergreen materials, and kept moist. Before the desert plant blooms fade, collect a few appealing specimens for the naturalized borders. But be sure to find out first which ones may be taken and which are protected by law.

Tubbed tropicals and subtropicals may now be restored to their summer patio sites. Get them used to the sun gradually, especially when they have been over-wintered in a rather dark room. You're advised to give even the most durable sun-lover a few weeks of light shade—a lath house or fencing is ideal—before exposing it to the full sun.

North from San Francisco, in the coastal zone, heaths and heathers may now be planted. But do not move the early spring-flowering varieties until they are done flowering. But the later-blooming heathers are best transplanted now. Be sure to maintain the original planting depth in the new site, and mulch all heaths with three to four inches of loose material that permits air to reach the roots.

North Pacific Coast gardeners should check their stored tuberous begonias for the pink sprouts that are due by now. Lay them three inches apart on flats filled with half peat moss and half sand or leaf mold. Keep moist, and when the sprouts are three to four inches long transfer to pots or the garden if the soil is warm enough.

If they haven't already done so, Coast gardeners should now plant some lily seeds in a cold frame or lath-covered nursery-bed, and transplant the young plants from last year's lily seeds to nursery rows.

The Orchard and Bush Fruits

Orchardists in all areas should check their apple trees by variety with the county agent or state ag bureau to see if they're self-pollinating. If your trees are not self-pollinating and you do not have cross-pollinators, plant some among them as soon as possible. Meanwhile, here's a thrifty habit which has produced emergency apples for many an orchardist: Borrow bouquets of good pollinators from a friendly neighbor, and place them in pails under the blossoming trees. Visiting bees will take care of the rest, going from the fresh bouquets to trees and back repeatedly.

However, for the future, bear in mind that bees do not work in windblown areas. If your fruit trees stand on an exposed site, you should be able to improve future yields by planting a windbreak. If you have started a windbreak, it may need a little protection to get it off to a sound start. Plant dense, fast-growing perennials, like golden-rod or St. John's-wort, that leave a stand of stalks over the winter to do the job for you. Any perennial that grows fast and strong in your area will do.

April's also the month in the central states to plant the shade tree seeds that were collected last fall. Situate them in a quiet corner of the nursery where they can rest undisturbed for as long as 24 to 36 months—it will take that long for some of them to germinate.

This is a good time to dust the soil under the fruit trees and grapevines with the wood ashes you've been saving from the winter fires. Their potash content will be used later in the manufacture of fruit sugar. While you're about it, spread nitrogen-rich fertilizers around the berry bushes and fruit trees, covering the fertilizer with a thick hay mulch, preferably alfalfa.

By now residents in Zones Three and Four should be able

to estimate the amount of winterkill their trees sustained in January and February. Many trees that died back to their roots will revive as shrubs if you give them the chance. Encourage them to make rapid growth with plenty of compost and moisture, but stop fertilizing them after the end of May. Then let them go dry in the fall, so the new growth will harden off by frost time. Keep in mind that they will need just as much protection next winter as they did when young.

Although it's precious, spread the remainder of your hoarded-up compost around your trees, shrubs, berry bushes and vines. Supplement it with high-nitrogen fertilizer such as blood meal, tankage, cottonseed meal or manure rich in nitrogen. But delay fertilizing the strawberries until after harvest, excepting those newly-planted rows that will not be allowed to set fruit this year.

All trees in Zones Two and Three—nut, fruit, shade and evergreen—should be given booster feedings. This can be done with an 18-inch-long earth auger hooked onto your power drill or with a deepfeeder on the end of your hoseline. We've done both, and prefer the deepfeeder which really gets the water down to the roots. Make the holes about nine inches to one foot apart under the dripline, and then fill them with compost (if you have any left) plus rock fertilizers and manure. Then mulch over with a good four-to-six-inch layer of hay, straw or wood chips that extends out to the dripline. If you use wood chips, be sure to add cottonseed or blood meal so you don't create nitrogen deficiency.

Evergreens may be pruned now on the West Coast when the new growth is well under way. Cut back no more than half the new growth to encourage a dense foliage. Finish pruning when the trees are still in their most active period.

Fruit and nut trees in the Southwest should be mulched—alfalfa hay is best. Ground corncobs are excellent for shrubs. Again, as with wood chips, add a nitrogen booster because the corncobs and chips make the soil bacteria work overtime. Evergreens should be pruned along the North Pacific shore, but with some care. Since future growth will all come from this year's growing tips, cut no more than a portion of the new growth on each branch, and prune only where necessary for shaping. Pruning must be done while the shoots are still in active growth.

Under Glass

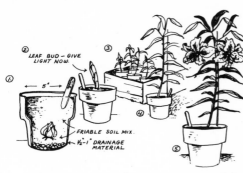

LEAF BUD - GIVE LIGHT NOW.

5"

FRIABLE SOIL MIX

½-1" DRAINAGE MATERIAL

1. PLANT AURATUM LILLIES IN DEEP 5" POTS. KEEP COOL AND DARK.
2. WHEN LEAF BUD APPEARS... BRING INTO LIGHT.
3. PLANTS MAY BE GROWN IN DEEP COLD FRAME UN- TIL IN BUD (4.)
5. DISPLAY IN PLACE OF HONOR FOR A TERRIFIC SEPTEMBER- OCTOBER SHOW.

Tomatoes, eggplant, peppers and lettuce planted last month or in February—Zones One and Two excepted—should be prepared now for outdoor planting. Separate and block out the roots by running a sharp kitchen knife through the soil between plants. It's best done one to two weeks before transplanting. During the last week gradually accustom the plants to outdoor conditions by exposing them to direct sunlight and wind for increasingly longer periods.

Head lettuce may be transplanted to the garden now in Zone Three. Early tomatoes can go out in Zone Four if you can give them good protection against last frosts. In Zones One and Two it's time to start seeds for the plants that will go outside in June. In Zone Three cabbage, broccoli, and cauliflower can safely be set outside.

Plant cucumbers, corn, melon, okra and squash in the open spaces left in the greenhouses by the departure to the garden of cold-hardy lettuce, broccoli and cabbage. They could all be started not too much later outdoors, but will make faster progress under glass for the first few weeks than they would in the row, and can be moved outside with practically no interrupted growth.

This is admittedly a gamble—many gardeners feel seeds planted a few weeks later in the outdoor row make up for lost time in their permanent site. But just as many believe that the plants make faster progress in those first few weeks under glass and that they lose no time or progress when pot-grown.

All the same, you're cautioned to watch the seedlings in the hotbeds and cold frames and also at the kitchen window so they don't grow "leggy." Keep thinning them and transplanting to prevent overcrowding.

Don't be too confident about the hardiness of potted Easter azaleas. Most of those sold for the holiday are tender and should be pampered. They should be well-watered and kept on a cool but cheerful windowsill and then set out in June under filtered sunlight by sinking the pots up to the rim. They will need some sunlight to make growth and blossoms and should be watered daily and then brought indoors before the first frost.

Meanwhile, if you have any time left over, the cold frame should be cleaned up now and made ready for the plants that you will be moving into it from now on right into early May —all part of the hardening-off process. Don't forget to water the plants regularly after you move them into the cold frame, and also be sure to open the sash a few inches or more in the warmer middle of the day.

However, until all danger of frost has passed by, your cold frame should be closed up tight for the night. When the weatherman gives the alert, cover the frame, as usual, with your collection of old blankets, comforters and burlap sacks— anything that keeps heat in and cold out.

Bear in mind that April does not mean a cessation of green- house activity—quite the contrary. The plants are no longer "resting," and the warmer, longer days mean more complete use of all food supplies—which means more waterings and feedings. We still like booster shots of organic liquid fish fertilizer, one tablespoon to a gallon of water.

Preparation for summer activity should also be well under way. Most February and many March cuttings will be rooted and ready for transfer to flats, bands or pots. Seedlings will now be large enough to handle, and should be transplanted. For ease in handling the annual vegetables and flowers, move them to smaller pans that hold 12 to 16 plants—they're handier than the larger and more clumsy wooden flats.

To grow your own achimenes, set eight to ten rooted corms that show two-to-three-inch growth in an eight or ten-inch bulb pan or hanging basket which should be lined with coarse, uncut sphagnum moss and filled with a general soil mixture, but without cow manure. Delay all feeding until the plants are well-developed and have started to bloom. Then feed with a liquid fertilizer (fish, one tablespoon to a gallon of water) every two weeks. Grow in the shaded part of the greenhouse or on a protected porch after all danger of frost has passed.

Lily bulbs should be placed in pots six inches or larger and completely covered with a soil mixture. Lilies potted this month for July-September bloom include Lilium auratum and Lilium rubrum for September-October show. The L. auratum bulbs should be in fresh and not cold storage. Place in a five-inch pot, and grow in a cool, 45-50-degree area, under the bench, in a cool cellar or a deep cold frame. Bring up to the light when a long leaf bud first appears—or later, if you prefer a long-stemmed plant.

Now's the time to take cuttings for fall and winter bloom of your fibrous-rooted begonias. The large-leaved varieties may be propagated from leaves by making several slits with a sharp knife or razor blade in the veins just below the branch division. Pin the leaf in moist sand with toothpicks, and water from below to avoid spattering the leaves which will rot if wet. When two or three small leaves appear and a root system is developing, separate from the parent leaf and shift to individual pots.

After the flowers of your Easter lily fade, it should be planted in the border where, with some care and good luck, it may send forth new bloom before frost. The spring-flowering bulbs should be turned out of their pots and planted with the soil balls undisturbed in the nursery where they will recover in a couple of years.

Philodendron cuttings—stem sections with two or more joints, terminal stem cuttings, or roots—will take hold in almost any medium, including water, and some of the larger varieties may be propagated by air-layering. Philodendron may also be grown from seeds that are sown as soon as they are ripe in a mixture of equal parts of sand and peat moss.

Annuals for the outdoor garden that may be sown this month include alyssum, phlox, snapdragon, baby's breath, chrysanthemums, cleome, marigolds, scabiosa, tithonia and zinnias for early blooms.

Cactus can be propagated now from the new growth. Cut off small, green pieces with a sharp knife, and allow them to dry and form a callus before potting. Christmas cherry which should be making new top growth, may be moved to a sunny place and given more water.

May
How Farming Began

Our debt to preliterate barbarians is heavy. Every single cultivated food plant of any importance has been discovered by some nameless barbarian society ... not only wheats and barleys, but rice, millet and maize, even yams, manioc, squashes or other plants that are not cereals at all.

What Happened in History
Gordon Childe

Farming began around 9,000 B.C. in what has since been called the "Fertile Crescent" which begins at the northern end of the Persian Gulf and then loops in a northwest direction with the Tigris and Euphrates Rivers to the swelling uplands. From these hills, the "Crescent" swings southwest to emerge on the shores of the Mediterranean, taking in the Holy Land and the Nile Valley and Delta.

This switch-over from nomadic barbarism to a primitive, though planned, economy where a man deliberately planted a crop because he assumed that both he and the crop would be around later for the harvest has changed the face of the world. From it has emerged, however painfully, culture and civilization, and society as we know it today.

But the heart of the question is—why did the first farming take place and when and where did it? We think the answers are to be found in a trio of source books which we recommend here unreservedly to the student of gardening. They are *Prehistoric Society* by Grahame Clark and Stuart Piggott [Pelican Book], *What Happened in History* by Gordon Childe [Pelican Book], and *World Prehistory* by Grahame Clark [Cambridge University Press].

The answer is manifest in the accompanying maps, which originally appeared in *Prehistoric Societies*. It is good to remember while studying them that by 9,000 B.C. the glaciers had completed a retreat from northern Europe, which started somewhere around 18,000 B.C. In the long process (short from the geological aspect) the Sahara became the desert it is today.

And now for the first of the maps—the distribution of wild sheep and goats. The range is quite wide, from the Bosphorus practically to the border of China, from the Persian Gulf clear up to the Caspian and Black Seas. But notice that the sheep and goats co-exist in a more reduced area, primarily the "Fertile Crescent."

A few words should be inserted here on what the continued presence of game and livestock must have meant to primitive man who was first a nomadic hunter. He followed herds in their seasonal migrations and later, when he had tamed the dog, he became a herdsman, tending and caring for the flocks, which turned out to be a symbiotic relationship, good for both man and beast.

Sheep and goats coexisted in a limited area, although their combined range was quite wide.

So man who had first raided and preyed off the herds of wild animals, killing and eating what he needed practically on the spot, learned to live peaceably with the animals, accustoming them to his continued presence, and leading them in time to their foothill pasturages. This, as far as we know, took place in the uplands of Asia Minor, somewhere between the Persian Gulf and the Caspian and Black Seas.

The range of wheat and barley was restricted to a much narrower region.

It is now time to consult our second map—the distribution of wild wheat and barley. Note that it follows even more narrowly the confines of the "Fertile Crescent." But note also that the spontaneous presence of wheat and barley overlap only in the region of Palestine and western Turkey.

So we find at Jericho a "perennial spring that would not only attract game and wild fowl, *but provide water for irrigation of small plots.* (Our italics.) The builders . . . hunted with slings and clubs . . . but they bred cattle, sheep and goats. They grew cereals by irrigation and reaped them with sickles of bone armed with flint teeth."

Were we to examine key sites in the transition to farming in southwest Asia the outlines of the "Crescent", would be unmistakable, swinging up the Tigris and Euphrates to the Anatolian uplands and then descending southward along the shores of the Mediterranean to Egypt. Reporting on the representative farming community of Jarmo in the year 7,000 B.C., Grahame Clark has this to say:

"It probably consisted of about 25 houses huddled together . . . constructed of packed mud, built up course by course. Clay ovens and the bases for silos were built into each house. . . . The villagers lived only to a slight extent by hunting . . . and depended mainly on mixed farming—two-rowed barley, emmer, spelt and peas were certainly cultivated, and sheep and goats were herded and maintained."

We know that cereals were harvested because the implements that did the work have been found; stone blades "showing the tell-tale gloss that came from friction with cornstalks, as well as milling stones, confirm that . . . cereals which we know were domesticated in the sense that they had been improved by breeding, and systemically sown."

And that's how things were almost 10,000 years ago when our gardening and farming ancestors first emerged from "preliterate barbarianism" into the beginnings of history. It is interesting to reflect that the world into which Jesus was born had a previous history of 7,000 years, more than three times as great as our own. In more than one sense, our society—and we—are older than we know.

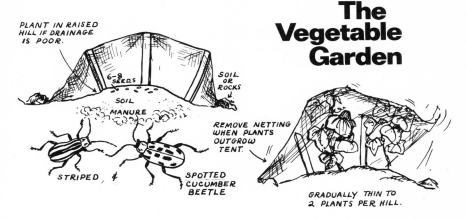

The
Vegetable
Garden

PLANT IN RAISED
HILL IF DRAINAGE
IS POOR.

6-8
SEEDS

SOIL
OR
ROCKS

SOIL

MANURE

REMOVE NETTING
WHEN PLANTS
OUTGROW
TENT.

STRIPED

SPOTTED
CUCUMBER
BEETLE

GRADUALLY THIN TO
2 PLANTS PER HILL.

Earliest planting date for the hardier crops such as broccoli in New Hampshire falls about on May 10. The really hardy crops like celery and lettuce can go in one week earlier, while the beans and summer squash should be planted one week later. The warm-weather crops—cucumbers, tomatoes, melons —can be set out toward the end of the month, from the 25th on.

In Connecticut, seeds of beans, Brussels sprouts, early and midseason cabbage may be planted, also carrots, cauliflower, chard, corn, cucumber, kohlrabi, muskmelons, lettuce, radishes, late potatoes, pumpkins, salsify, spinach and turnips. Transplant globe artichokes, beans, cabbage, kohlrabi, kale, leek, lettuce, muskmelons, onions, peppers and squash.

Tomatoes can be set out now in Zone Three and in most parts of Zones One and Two, but keep a supply of protective hotcaps on hand. Bushel or half-bushel baskets are fine if you don't have the styrofoam. But without protective measures such as these, you'll do best to wait until the frosts have retreated.

If you persist, keep the tomatoes covered until the thermometer stays well above the 50-mark. Wrap cutworm collars on tender young stems including peppers, Malabar spinach, eggplant and okra unless, like us, you start your seedlings in metal cans which become absolutely perfect cutworm protection in the outdoors.

71

From the beginning of the month, spinach, sweet corn, bush and pole beans may be planted in Rhode Island while cantaloupes, squash, watermelons, tomatoes go in starting on May 10, and eggplants and peppers from May 15.

In New York, plant soy beans, squash, cucumbers, successive head lettuce, parsley, radishes, eggplant, peppers and tomatoes. Summer squash may be planted in New Jersey around May 1; peppers, tomatoes and sweet potatoes on May 15. Pennsylvania gardeners can plant beans from May 1 as well as sweet corn, onion seeds and plants. Soybeans may go in from May 10 to 25; midseason cabbage until May 10, with lettuce, mustard, spinach, beets throughout the month. Begin with the sweet potatoes and tomatoes about May 20.

Have you laid in a good supply of netting or cheesecloth for planting cucumbers, melons and squash? Their seeds can go in as soon as you're sure the frosts have departed permanently. Set a cheesecloth or net tent over each hill, and leave it in place until the growing vines lift it up off the ground. With a little luck or good management, the tents should help you outwit the cucumber beetle.

Succession plantings of snap bush beans, beets and sweet corn can start in Delaware, plus the first planting of squash. From May 10 to 15 pole limas, pepper plants, radishes, sweet corn and canning tomatoes, either for the first or succession crops, should be started.

May is the month for the tender vegetables in Virginia, including okra, sweet potato, tomatoes, watermelons, cantaloupes and peppers. It's getting rather late for peas, but kale may still be sown. In Kentucky, it's time to start the canning tomatoes, late cabbage, broccoli, and Brussels sprouts in an outside bed.

Until the middle of the month in Tennessee plant celery, cucumbers, salsify, okra and early tomatoes. Corn may be planted for the entire month, and New Zealand spinach during the second half.

Give each plant a generous drink of manure water when setting it out to get it off to a fast start. Eggplant and okra should be given additional manure water every week or ten days throughout the season. But don't overfeed the tomatoes because the extra nitrogen will delay ripening.

Asparagus cutting should be at its rewarding height in most of the northern sectors. After six weeks' cutting, allow the plants to make tops which will manufacture the food for next year's crop.

Crowder peas can be planted down South as a cover crop, as food for the table—or as both. Plant them 30 pounds to the acre, if your soil needs building up. But if you have sandy soil—try crotalaria which is the better soil-restorer.

Staking or training of tomatoes can begin as soon as the plants grow heavy. But keep in mind that the professional growers in Virginia seem to get best results from tomatoes grown in wire cylinders which saves them the trouble of staking and tieing. In any case, keep the fruit from touching the soil if you want a high-vitamin count and minimum end-rot.

South Georgia can still put in bush, pole and lima beans, while middle-of-the state gardeners can work with cabbage, cucumbers, okra, pepper, squash, tomato plants and watermelons. Beans, beets, carrots, parsnips, peas, peppers, radishes, spinach, tomatoes, turnips and watermelons should be started now in the northern sections. In central Alabama it's time to sow Spanish peanuts, and Rokuson soybeans should be planted by the middle of the month. Okra and corn can be planted out in Louisiana, also cucumbers and field peas in the northern parts. It's too late to do much planting in Florida at this time except for summer squash and sweet potatoes in the northern parts.

Up in the broad Zone Three belt, May 15th is the date when beans start to be planted out in Ohio, also cucumbers and the warm-weather crops. Throughout the month, beets, carrots, sweet corn, kale, summer squash and turnips may go out, while tomatoes, peppers and sweet potatoes are planted during the third week. About the same timetable will apply to northern Illinois while gardeners in the south sectors will plant beets, carrots and cucumbers early in the month, also limas, muskmelons, peppers and snap beans.

After the frosts are over in Michigan, warm-weather crops can be started including corn, beans, radishes and leaf lettuce while tomatoes, eggplant and peppers may be set out, too. May is the month in Minnesota when most garden crops go into the open: chard, sweet corn and New Zealand spinach early in the month; beans, cucumbers and pumpkins by the middle. Approximate date for bush beans in Madison, Wisconsin, is May 10th; for early cabbage, cauliflower and lettuce plants, May 1st; while the warm-weather crops are planted out about May 20.

Asparagus can be planted on May 1 in North Dakota, while vine crops, planted in berry boxes about April 20 in Nebraska, may be put out when all danger from frost is past. Mulching with straw about May 10-20 should bring good results.

Since many counties have their last killing frost this month in Idaho, the half-hardy crops may be planted out now while the tender vegetables should be held back until all danger is safely past. As for the very tender summer vegetables, wait until the soil is thoroughly warmed. In Utah the cool-weather crops like carrots may still be sown. The beans and other tender crops like tomatoes can be planted after May 10, while the very tender ones—limas, cucumbers, canteloupes, pepper, squash and watermelon—wait until after the middle of the month.

Along California's northern coast, it's time for the limas, beets, cantaloupes, pepper and tomato plants, cucumbers, sweet potatoes and pumpkins between May 1-15. Along the southern coast, plant limas, more beets, summer and winter squash, tomatoes, sweet potatoes, melons, peppers and radishes. Beans, limas, sweet corn, cucumbers, okra, tomato, and pepper plants may be set out in the interior valleys, Imperial and Coachella excepted.

Bush beans may be planted from May 1 to July 15 in Oregon; corn through the month until June 15; pole beans, limas, summer squash, cucumbers and pumpkins through the second week of the month. In the south central section of Washington Early Wonder and Detroit Dark Red Beets may be planted successfully, also broccoli, Chantenay carrots, pickling and slicing cucumbers, endive, kohlrabi, spinach, sweet corn and tomatoes. In the western zones plant Nantes carrots, head lettuce, broccoli, sweet corn and turnips. In the northeastern parts work with Danish Ball head cabbage, Chantenay carrots, cauliflower, leaf lettuce, sweet corn and tomatoes. Save cantaloupes and watermelons for the last part of the month.

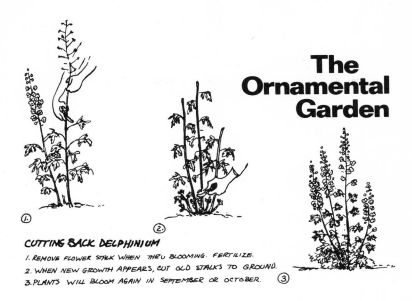

The Ornamental Garden

CUTTING BACK DELPHINIUM

1. REMOVE FLOWER STALK WHEN THRU BLOOMING. FERTILIZE.
2. WHEN NEW GROWTH APPEARS, CUT OLD STALKS TO GROUND.
3. PLANTS WILL BLOOM AGAIN IN SEPTEMBER OR OCTOBER.

We didn't have too much snow in Pennsylvania this winter, and if there isn't a little excess rain in store for us this summer, the soil can dry considerably. Nevertheless, let's start by keeping the mulch well away from the rows, beds, and borders which will give the sun a chance to warm things up properly. But keep your leaves, old straw, hay and what-have-you handy so you can haul it back into place after the soil has warmed up.

In general, it's always sound practice to have the mulch ready as the days grow longer and the sun comes further and further north. Try to remember how much snow covered your garden this past winter and how long it remained on each occasion. This should be your guide in mulching matters this year. Right now, thanks to April, the earth should be saturated in all but a very few areas; so the soil should be given a chance to absorb some light and air.

As soon as the night frosts are safely over plant out the seedlings you started indoors. Unless it sends up a main flower spike like snapdragon or stocks, pinch back the growing tip of each plant. Start hardening off the annuals that are in the cold frame or on the windowsill. The half-hardy annuals can be seeded in the borders now, but wait until the earth is lima-bean warm before sowing the zinnias or nasturtiums.

This month in the northern and eastern parts of the country

almost invariably gives the gardener the "go-ahead" signal for sowing the seeds of the tender annuals, plus for the setting-out of the half-hardy seedlings or long-season annuals.

If large flower heads are desired, the soil should be well-fertilized with compost for your zinnias, asters, calendula and the African marigolds. All of these will do well enough in leaner soil, but their blooms will naturally be smaller.

Play it safe, and keep a garden plan on hand while planting annuals in the borders. Otherwise, you may injure those perennials that have not yet come up.

Take care when shifting the long-season annuals from the seed flats to the garden not to destroy their roots. It may be necessary to protect the tender transplants from the direct rays of the sun for a few days until new roots capable of absorbing water from the soil are formed. Pinch out the central bud at the top of each plant when it is six inches high to obtain stocky growth. Among those that will benefit from this treatment are ageratum, calendula, marigolds, Drummond's phlox, petunias, snapdragons, stocks and sweet alyssum.

Now's the time to sow perennial seeds for next year's garden. The young plants will be ready to be set in the garden either in the fall or early next spring. Some of the perennials will bloom a second time when the old stems are cut down after the first period of bloom is over—particularly delphinium and achillea. New stems will grow out to bear bloom in September or October, thus adding variety to your garden's color. Among the more rewarding plants are anemones, asters, boltonias, chrysanthemums, delphiniums, lilies and phlox.

Don't forget to give the rock garden plants a generous dressing of compost. The peonies should also be fed at this time because they are forming the flowers that will open later this month or early next month.

In the central states peonies should be disbudded now for bigger blooms. Since the secondary buds sometimes produce only small flowers, remove all but the plumpest bud from each stalk. Don't fail to give the plants a side-dressing of wood ashes or granite dust to ensure better blooms next year, and give each plant a good drink of manure water after disbudding.

It's also the time further south to enjoy your spring garden to its fullest. But be sure your soil has an extra-adequate supply of humus so it will hold plenty of moisture against the hot summer days. As soon as the spring bloom is over, remove the plants and spade up the bed to get it ready for your summer annuals. The compost pile should benefit from all garden wastes and plant residues.

Mulch the azaleas with oak leaves, and plant dahlias about the middle of the month for fall bloom. For masses of color, plant your favorite variety of African marigold or large-flowered zinnias. Bear in mind, while you're about it, that the French marigolds are particularly effective against nematodes. So, if you haven't already done so, start some now and keep adding to them if you want to keep your soil free of nematode trouble.

Chrysanthemums should be pinched back in the Southwest, and the treatment continued every two weeks until July. (Consult the schedule that appears in this month's "Under Glass" section.) Remove the faded flowers from the bulbs and perennials before they go to seed. Since the bulbs should be given a rest, allow their beds to go somewhat dry unless they have been interplanted with annuals. Any time from now to July is suitable for rooting rhododendrons from cuttings.

Bone meal and wood ashes should be spread around the spring-flowering bulbs. Allow the leaves to yellow before you cut them back. Where daffodil leaves have been crowding the annual seedlings, tie them into clumps after the flowers have faded.

Cut the seedpods off the lilacs, but do not prune the stems. When the bushes are growing too tall, cut back a few trunks with the ground each year until the whole bush is shortened. This method will also provide good results with Philadelphus, Kolkwitzia and others which have a tendency to grow too leggy.

Late-blooming lilies can be lifted and divided at this time. Before you dig up the plants, prepare new sites because the fleshy roots should not be allowed to dry out. Get your soil test kit and determine if the pH in the new site matches that in the old where they have flourished. Also, make sure they have perfect drainage in their new home.

This is the month in Zones Two and Three when the flowering shrubs come into their own and reward you for your skill and patience. Among these are the rhododendrons and azaleas, the lilac, flowering crabs and cherries, and wisteria. Feed the plants just before and during the flowering period, and remember to remove the old flowers as soon as the blossoms have faded.

The tulips should be given some extra care after the blooming period to make sure they replenish their food supplies in anticipation of next year's growth and blooms. But do not disturb the bed until the leaves are brown and the stems have dried out. To hide the fading plants and brighten the border, set out annuals.

Don't forget to pay some attention to the natural flower gardens that will abound in woodside meadows and hilltops. Here in eastern Pennsylvania we were lucky enough to find a dampish, wild half-acre where the woods ended and the meadow began. From it—with the owner's permission—we carefully removed skunk cabbages, May apples and Jack-in-the-pulpit which we set out on the shady east side of the house, under the trees and next to the pond where they flourished handsomely. But take what you can get and find in your area. There's the marsh marigold, a succulent that grows in wet places with large buttercup-like flowers; the hepaticas with their three-lobed leaves and subtly tinted white, pinkish or bluish flowers; trilliums with red or white-tinged pink flowers, and trailing arbutus with its pinkish and fragrant flowers (Remember that, like the azalea and rhododendron, it likes acid soils.). Learn about these free-for-the-taking natural beauties—they are worth your time and attention and can add interest and variety to the grounds.

The Orchard and Bush Fruits

PEACHES

THINNING FRUIT

PLUMS

May is the month to spread nitrogen-rich fertilizers around the woody ornamentals, fruit trees, grapevines and berry bushes. Use any nitrogen-rich material that is abundant, free or cheap—and mature—in your section. A thick layer of rotted wood chips, manure or sawdust, plus a heavy dusting of cottonseed or blood meal is fine, also generous applications of tankage or sludge. Be sure to feed all woody plants in time to give the new growth plenty of days in which to harden.

Check with your local municipal sewage-treatment plant to find if sludge is available for the taking. Try to use a plain pickup truck if possible, one with a metal bed and frame that can be hosed out at the end of the chore. Treat the sludge just as you would any soil additive, running it out to the drip lines and hilling it in under the bushes. If it has caked at the municipal plant, you may have to screen it or run it once through the shredder. But it should assay at two to three percent nitrogen, and farmers who have used it once have come back for more. Try it.

The daily cleanup of fruit from under the apple, peach and plum trees is the best form of protection against insects you can practice. So throughout May and June bury the fallen fruit immediately in an active compost heap, getting it right in the center of the pile. John Keck collects all fallen apples at the Organic Gardening Experimental Farm and carefully deposits them on top of a circular pile of leaves which is at least six feet wide at the top and about three feet high.

The top of the mound is as flat and stable as a pancake and can hold great quantities of fallen fruit safely where they decompose and heat up, killing all the larvae present. This is most important, so be sure to bury your windfalls in a compost pile that's active—really steaming. Come July, you may be able to cook some of the fallen fruit.

Fungus growths that attack peaches and plums can occur if May is wetter than usual in your area. Their spread can be discouraged if not prevented by sprinkling lime or wood ashes under the trees. Peaches and plums should be thinned after the spring drop. Allow four to six inches between the peaches, and three inches between the plums for the best size.

Nursery cuttings of grapes should be given plenty of water, and then mulched generously. In the hotter, more southerly areas, cuttings may require some extra protection from the light—lath fencing is fine.

Watch the peach and apricot trees for signs of gummosis which can be the oozing of thick, gummy matter through the bark or spontaneous wounds. Again, pick and compost all fallen and mummified fruit, and nurse the affected trees with booster feedings of aged manure and liquid fish fertilizer diluted one tablespoon to the gallon. After July 1, discontinue feeding until time to resume massive applications of fish fertilizer in the late fall when all danger of delayed growth resulting in tender wood is past.

After they have finished blooming, the early-flowering shrubs should be pruned and given a mulch of strawy, rotted manure. The peonies should be disbudded now for bigger blooms, removing all but the thickest bud from each stalk. (The secondary buds all too often produce small flowers, and occasionally are completely blasted.) While you're at it, be sure to give all plants a side dressing of wood ashes or granite dust to improve next year's blooms.

The peaches and plums should be thinned after the spring drop. Allow four to six inches between the peaches, and three inches between the plums for the best size. If the month has been wetter than usual, discourage the spread of fungus by sprinkling ground limestone or wood ashes under the trees.

Under Glass

SANSEVERIA CUTTINGS

NEW PLANT

ROOTING IN WATER

CUT OFF OLD LEAF.

3-4" SECTIONS OF LEAF ROOT IN MOIST SAND IN ABOUT 4 WEEKS.

You've got plenty to do now that the days are warmer and longer, but do not be in too much of a hurry if you live in Canada and Zone Two or even Zone Three because killing frosts can nip the annuals and perennials you have moved out to the garden. Also bear in mind that the nights can stay on the cool side for the rest of the month if the weather is unseasonable.

When you do move your plants, leave most of them in their pots which should be sunk in the ground up to their rims. Aluminum foil wrapped around the pot will keep the moisture inside while it prevents invasion by unwelcome soil inhabitants. Continue your usual precautions of knowing the shade-and-light needs of your different plants when working outdoors, and keep a record of where the plants have been placed. If you are conscientious, no plants will be missed in feeding or watering, and nobody will be left outside in the fall.

As the plants are moved outside, make the most of the opportunity to tidy up the benches and tables and wet down the aisles and under the benches, as needed. Except on dull, wet days, the plants should be given water daily. It's also time to take the humidifier out of the bedroom and install it in the greenhouse where it will be greatly needed over the summer.

The cold frame will get a chance now to earn its keep by sheltering the seedlings you started in March and April. They should be ready now for pots, flats or bands pending their eventual transfer to the garden.

House ferns that were dormant during the winter may be making new growth now. You should either repot them, or remove the top inch of soil from their pots, replacing it with your richest compost.

Repot the azaleas every year or two before shifting to the garden. After removing the old topsoil and that about the root system carefully, replace with a mixture of equal parts of aged cow manure, acid leafmold (from oaks) and peat moss. Set the plants so they get the early morning sun but are protected for the rest of the day, and water daily unless there is rain. Prune the plants at repotting time to give them a good shape.

When replanting your geraniums in the garden, bear in mind that while the zonal varieties will prosper in both sun or semi-shade, the fancy-leaved varieties will not tolerate direct sunlight, and so should be set out in a shaded area. If the geranium foliage becomes somewhat reddened, a lack of nitrogen may be the cause. Feed daily with liquid fish fertilizer (one tablespoon to the gallon) until the condition is rectified.

The snapdragons may be cut back when they have finished

blooming and set out in the garden. Many gardeners report these transplants actually make a better outside display than those originally sown for the outdoor garden.

The hardy chrysanthemums that were brought in from the cold frame in March or April should now show new growth for cuttings. They will root in any medium with 60-to-65-degree bottom heat and should be ready for potting or setting out in the garden in about three weeks. Some kind of shading should be provided every day at 5 p.m. and removed at 8 a.m. It can be heavy opaque paper or a black cloth. With individual pots, a large, dark paper bag may be used. A typical chrysanthemum cutting-planting schedule for large single specimen blooms is as follows: Take cuttings—May 15; plant—June 5; pinch—June 26; begin shading—July 31; begin bloom—Oct. 2. The schedule for pompom or mass blooms is as follows: take cuttings—May 5; plant—May 26; first pinch—June 16; second pinch—July 7; last pinch and shading—July 28; begin bloom—Sept. 29.

Well after the last frost date has passed, tuberous begonias can be removed to the shaded porch or sunk in pots in the ground on the shaded part of the garden. Shift to six- or eight-inch pots before setting them out under the trees, or set them on the north side of the house near a wall or a dense hedge. The trailing varieties will do well hanging in baskets on the porch, in shaded window boxes, or suspended from trees. They should be fed once every two weeks with a low-nitrogen fertilizer.

Sanseveria leaves may be rooted in water, or a leaf may be cut into three-to-four-inch lengths and inserted in moist sand with the base-end down. New plants will grow from the base of the leaf in about four weeks. Pot up the old leaf and the new plant in a four-inch pot containing a general soil mixture. Cut off the old leaf when the new plant establishes itself satisfactorily.

Keeping an eye on that last frost date for your area, start to prepare your window boxes for the summer. A good working soil mixture that will accommodate most plants consists of two parts loam, one part sand, compost, leaf mold or sludge. It's a good practice to add one trowelful of bone meal or wood ashes to each box. An eight-by-eight-by-36-inch box will take about one bushel of soil.

After the plants are set, mulch with peat moss or buckwheat hulls, although the latter may blow about if set at a window on the exposed side. Put the plants in a little closer than you would at the border, and keep them well pinched back. Place the vines on the outside; the small, erect plants in the middle, and the tallest plants nearest the window. Work with plants that are suited to the amount of sun they will receive in the various exposures. Southern window boxes should contain only plants that can stand a great deal of heat, unless the window boxes will not bloom much; foliage plants will do better on that side of the house.

Boxes on the south and west sides can best be planted with geraniums, English ivy, coleus, marigold, lantana, verbena, alyssum and impatiens. East sills that get only the morning sun can support some ferns, German ivy, fuchsia, Kenilworth ivy, vinca, nasturtiums, petunias and tuberous begonias. The north side will be best for the asparagus fern, Boston fern, caladiums, croton, ground ivy, morning glory, trailing vinca and petunias.

Except for the still uncertain Zones One and Two, window-sill plants may now be moved to their outdoor summer places. Filtered sun or shade from 11 a.m. to 4 p.m. are recommended if you want to move everything outside—African violets and philodendrons excepted. Keep in mind that the only house plants that can handle the full summer sun all day long are the cacti, the succulents and possibly the geraniums. They will all suffer less shock when you harden them off gradually.

Leave the plants in their pots—it's easier to bring them in later if you do. But sink them in the soil all the way up to the rims to keep them moist. Some may require repotting, and bear in mind that all will require more water outdoors than they did inside.

Most of the vegetable seedlings will be removed this month from the greenhouse and cold frame, and a thorough cleaning should be done at this time. Clean up as you empty the benches, and get your fall flowers and tomatoes started. If you're looking forward to fall—even winter—bloom, start Christmas cherry, aster, acacia, Christmas pepper, cineraria and fibrous-rooted begonias now.

June
Harvesting Vegetables in a Drought

I love to hoe in the early morning with only the birds and me to keep company with the rising sun. It is so peaceful, and everything is damp with sweet-smelling dew. I love it.

Jennie Hutton

Start mulching now, wherever you are. Here's why:

"June 15th and no rain. Hot sun coming out steady. Strawberries look good yet. I pack water by the pail to tomato and cabbage plants Mondays, Wednesdays and Fridays. Strawberries get a drink on Tuesdays and Thursdays. Half of the cabbage left, 100 plants. Three-fourths of the tomatoes, about 40 plants and only 200 strawberry plants. One bucket of water dampens six plants, so it is a real chore watering them, but I hate to see them die.

"June 20th and no rain. Garden is burning bad. I woke up the other morning, and something had eaten all the cabbage off. Tomatoes are struggling hard for survival. July first, and still the hot, dry winds. July 15th, the same. One mess of peas, and the vines are gone.

"All I harvested after heat and insects had taken their toll were eight strawberries, a gallon of tomatoes with large dry-rot spots on all, three cucumbers, one mess of peas and sweet corn; no beets, radishes or lettuce for two weeks; carrots the size of threads, one mess of onions, two midget melons and four small pumpkins. This, which should feed eight people through to the next bearing season, wouldn't keep one."

The above story of almost unrelieved garden disaster was sent to us some time ago by Jennie Hutton from the dry-land corner of southeastern Montana. Confronted with minimum rainfall and hot, burning winds, she reckoned correctly that gardens and crops were gambles—unless you mulched and composted. Mrs. Hutton also noted that her large family—six children and two adults—made the garden a necessity—it was the only economical way to feed her brood.

But what was she to do after a disastrous year gave them nothing to add to the family larder? For six out of ten years her gardens had hailed out or burned up. The four so-called "good" years had yielded sufficient crops but, in order to create a real surplus, Mrs. Hutton had to put in a large patch.

She'd heard talk about the organic method with its then far-fetched and new-fangled idea of mulching to conserve soil moisture. But would it work in her hot, dry and ever-windy country? She decided to find out by trying it. The next spring, "after April made its showery entrance," she began her grand experiment. On top of the still-damp garden soil she spread a shallow layer of poultry manure, all hauled in by the barrowful and unloaded by hand. She also spread some rotted alfalfa hay which she cleaned out of last winter's feedlot, and had it plowed.

After waiting out a snowstorm that held up all garden work for three full weeks, she put in 300 strawberry plants and then, increasing the garden area even further, she planted the garden "all at the same time as the season was far advanced."

One week later, after resting her aching back she spread some old alfalfa hay on the strawberries, placing them between rows all the way "until all you could see was green plants and old yellow hay." Next she set out 300 cabbages and 200 tomato plants—not exactly a light chore. Some friends inquired affectionately and ironically if she "intended to supply the United States." But, she added, "they knew as well as I how many usually survived."

As the season progressed, "everything came up on schedule, including the sun." There were a few rains which were welcome, but, as the plants grew larger Jennie Hutton took no chances and mulched between the rows with more of the baled alfalfa. Sure enough, the days came on hotter and hotter while the wind "blew its continuous wail." She watered the 300 cabbages and 200 tomato plants, but the job proved too backbreaking—"there were just too many of them," she admitted. However, her reward was close at hand.

Came another June and this time her garden looked "wonderful, although the crops in this area are burning badly." She reported not seeing "an insect and weeds are very few." While a hard wind blew the hotcaps off the tomato and cabbage plants, the cutworms never bothered them.

By the end of July the Hutton countryside was still without rain. But her garden—thanks to the organic preparation and the sustained mulching she gave it was "the best I have ever seen in this part of the country—*raised without benefit of water.*" (Our italics) But what about the results—in addition to the good looks? Here they are: She canned 400 pints of peas, 300 quarts of tomatoes, 100 quarts of juice, 200 quarts of vegetables and fruits, and still had "a great surplus for the neighbors." Strawberries planted in the spring (300 plants) averaged one pint per plant.

Is there a moral in all this for us more favored gardeners who don't have to contend with steady, hot, dry winds and a remorseless sun? There is—"the ground between the plants was still moist under the mulch after a record hot summer," she reports. Also, for a clincher, she worked with the same seeds and with varieties she had used before, so "I know it was the manure and mulch that did it," she stresses.

Finally: "My greatest blessing was to see three cynical neighbors change their minds—and all are out now for the organic way. I only wish everyone would do the same," she concluded.

THIN TO
2 PLANTS
PER HILL.

SQUASH & MELONS

The Vegetable Garden

IF BORERS ATTACK— ROOTED VINES
WILL CARRY ON.

COVER RUNNER WITH SOIL
AT LEAF NODES.

It's getting time to apply mulch as the sun gets higher in the sky and the ground warms up. Up to now we have held back on the straw, hay, leaves—what-have-you? because comparative plantings at the Experimental Farm have shown that late mulching pays off with tomatoes and other warm-weather crops. So out comes the shredder and last year's crop residues go through it along with any early spring weeds we've permitted to grow. From now on, unless the weather is rainy as it has not been for the last ten years hereabouts, we mulch progressively. If you haven't a shredder, you can chop your way through the above materials using a rotary mower—set it high, at three inches.

Gardens in Zone One should be ready. Lettuce, onion sets, potatoes, carrots, radishes, kohlrabi and escarole may be planted first, while summer squash, bush beans, zucchini, sweet corn and cucumbers can go in by mid-month when the nights will be warmer.

Plant corn, peppers, late potatoes, tomatoes, bush beans and pickling cucumbers. Again, any mulch that was pulled back to allow the soil to warm up should be replaced now. Pole and lima beans may be planted, and eggplant set out. It's a good idea to plant an extra row of carrots now for Zone Three's coming winter.

When it's one foot high, side-dress the first corn planting with rich compost or cottonseed meal. Plant sweet potatoes in Zone Three, and start seeds in flats for late plantings of cabbage, celery, cauliflower and Brussels sprouts in Zones Two and Three.

Zones Four and Five residents should thin melons to one or two plants per hill and, as the squash and melon vines spread, throw a handful or soil over each runner at two or three leaf nodes. The extra roots that grow from these points may later save the vines if borers attack the first roots. As the bush summer squash starts to bloom, plant a few more hills—they will be ready to bear when the first plantings begin to slow.

Some shade should be provided for tomatoes in the drier parts of Zones Four and Six both for good color and extra vitamins. While you're being active, now's the time to protect lettuce with netting and/or laths—snow fencing is ideal—which will help prevent bolting. Lettuce can also be interplanted among small trees which will provide just about the right amount of shading. But further south and west the rows should be well-watered and mulched and the sunshades in place. Make sure heading lettuce has good ventilation and growing room—the heads rot quickly in hot weather.

Second plantings of sweet corn and bush beans may be made now in Zone Two, while limas may now be planted in all but the coldest areas. Use pea pods to mulch the asparagus beds, keeping the bed well-weeded until the stalks grow dense enough to choke out the weeds.

Properly renovated after each harvest, strawberry beds should last for years. As soon as the pickings dwindle, dig out all of the woody old plants. Spread an inch of rich compost around the remaining vital young plants; mulch the paths heavily with clean straw, and draw the mulch up to the plants. As new runners develop, tuck the most promising under the mulch, and cut off the rest. If you have a hunch that your compost is low in nitrogen, spike it with a booster of blood meal or cottonseed meal before spreading.

If your matted rows have spread out and filled the paths, you can work over the bed easily by running your rotary mower right down the center of the old rows, leaving the young plants in the paths to carry on for next year. This may leave a few bald patches which can be made right next month when you train new runners into the bare areas.

If you started working with wire cylinders or row-long tent racks, you should start reaping a bonus of rot-free tomatoes shortly. In any event, let your tomato plants sprawl in the sun if you insist, but keep the fruit off the ground. We've used triangular wire racks for years, set between the rows and under the plants. The row-long frames, about 15-18 inches tall, keep the fruit up and also let light and air in around the plants which can be important because too-dense greenery can promote fungus attacks.

Down south, seedlings should be kept coming along in the vacated vegetable rows. You can raise an extra summer crop of collards, mustard, zucchini, and bush beans before you plant the winter vegetables in their rows.

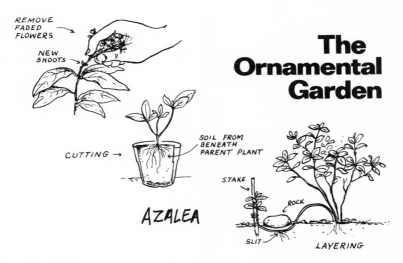

REMOVE FADED FLOWERS

NEW SHOOTS

CUTTING →

SOIL FROM BENEATH PARENT PLANT

AZALEA

STAKE

ROCK

SLIT

LAYERING

The Ornamental Garden

Everything in the ornamentals should be under mulch by now in Zones Three through Seven while mulch should be spread now in Zone Two. Fresh-ground corncobs are fine for roses while coffee grounds mixed with an inch of sawdust, make a satisfactory flower-bed mulch. But be sure with the corncobs and sawdust to add some nitrogen in the form of cottonseed or soybean meal. Under the shrubbery, the coarser screenings from the compost pile may be spread loosely.

The seedheads on all perennials should be removed and the plants cut back, first to half-height, later to the crown in order to obtain bloom later in the year. The roses should be well-watered and mulched, except where heavy rains encourage fungous growths.

Biennial and perennial seeds should be started now for next year's garden in Zones One, Two and Three. Rambler roses in Zones Three and Four should be cut back when they are done blooming.

Gardeners in all zones should prune the spring-flowering shrubs when they have finished blooming. The heaths should be well-mulched with pine needles or oakleaf mold, and pruned only where a shoot gets out of line.

Spring-flowering shrubs in the central states should be pruned as they finish blooming, and the spring perennials cut back as the flowers fade. But do not cut back the foliage from peonies when removing the seed pods, and do not permit fancy hybrid seeds to ripen and self-sow, because their offspring may not come true. Rambler roses should be cut back after blooming, removing the weaker new canes and also all those that bore flowers.

Roses in Zone Two should be fed liquid manure or fish fertilizer, and mulched with buckwheat or cocoa bean shells or ground corncobs. Add some extra nitrogen—cottonseed or soybean meal—if you use the corncobs.

After their leaves turn yellow lift any spring-flowering bulbs that are too crowded. Divide and replant daffodils and narcissus, and store tulips in a cool, dry place until autumn. Trim lupines all the way to the ground after they have flowered, and cut delphiniums half-way back now, later cutting them to their crowns after the second flowering. Unless you want volunteers next year, remove and compost biennials before they scatter their seed.

When they are finished blooming, iris should be divided and transplanted. Discard the woody centers of the plants, and replant the vigorous outer tubers, each with one or two fans of leaves which should be shortened to four or five inches.

Delphiniums should be cut half-way back when they have ended blooming to encourage second flowering. After the second flowers have faded, cut the stalks back to the crown.

Geraniums should not be overwatered at this time—they will bloom best when kept somewhat dry. However, the azaleas, camellias and roses should be kept well-watered as the weather turns hot. Watch roses for shoots sprouting below the graft, and rub them out before the fancy varieties revert to their rootstock parents.

Autumn crocus should be planted now further south. Where they are crowded, dig and divide iris, after blooming. The azaleas, magnolias, jasmine and camellias—the woody ornamentals—may be propagated by layering this month. Bend down a lower branch, cutting or slitting it slightly on its lower side, and bury the wounded limb in the soil, allowing the leaves at its end to remain above ground. Pin the branch in place firmly with a wire hoop or rock, and by next spring you should have a newly-rooted plant.

Palms, yucca and bamboo may be transplanted this month in the lower South. The plants should be mulched well, and staked against the wind. Hibiscus cuttings can be taken as soon as the new growth turns woody. Keep them shaded and moist until they send up new shoots.

Southwest gardeners should replace the early annuals and spring bulbs with such heat-tolerant annuals as marigolds, cosmos, annual phlox, zinnias, tithonia and gaillardias. Tuberous begonias should be watered every two weeks with liquid manure. After they finish blooming, trim and prune tree peonies, and mulch them along with the clematis and chrysanthemums with rich compost or rotted manure.

Continue to pinch back chrysanthemums in all areas. Allow the shoots to grow six inches long when making cuttings, nipping just below a leaf node. Strip off all the leaves except the end one, and thrust the denuded stems into a moist but sandy loam. They should be ready for transplanting within one month.

Keep in mind that the marigolds—the French and Aztec varieties especially—are still recommended as a sovereign cure for soil nematodes. But it takes more then one season of continuous planting to build up enough of the substance that drives the nematodes away, so you should make repeated plantings throughout the garden—including the vegetable patch—if you have not already done so.

Geraniums should not be overwatered at this time. They will bloom best when kept somewhat dry.

Azaleas should have their faded blooms removed on the West Coast, but only the flowers. New branches will come from the axils just below the flower stems and, if you want to propagate them, take cuttings of well-ripened wood, and start them in soil taken from beneath the mother plant. Or, you can layer a likely branch by bending it over and pinning it to the ground. The best time for doing this is between now and August 15.

This is the time, south of the Bluegrass Line in Zones Four through Seven to start lawns. Be sure to work in as much organic matter as possible before planting. Best varieties for these areas are Bermudagrass, carpetgrass and centipede-grass. They may be sown from seeds or sprigs, but zoysia or St. Augustinegrass must be sprigged.

Keep the old lawns at the three-inch level in the dry areas of Zones Three and Four. Water in the morning or early part of the afternoon, never in the late evening. If your region is suffering the fungus turf diseases, close cutting and vigorous raking may help in the wetter parts.

The Orchard and Bush Fruits

After the sterile fruits have fallen in the Zone Two annual drop, thin the remaining crops on the apple, peach, plum and prune trees. Remove all but one fruit from each cluster, and space the apples and peaches at four-to-eight-inch intervals, allowing the plums and prunes one to three inches. The wider spacing is allowed the earlier varieties.

Keep the fallen fruit picked up and composted, and compost the thinnings as well. If you do not have a heap that is heating up, build one now—infested fruit should go into an active compost pile to destroy pests and diseases. Circular heaps of composting leaves at the Organic Experimental Farm are used to take care of such fruit. Measuring six feet across at the top and standing more than three feet high, they contain the composting apples safely until disease and pests cannot escape or spread from such enclosures.

This is the time to protect the peach and plum trees from borers. To do a thorough and effective job, remove the soil around the base of the tree to a depth of three inches. Then bind the trunk of the tree with painter's masking tape in a snug sheath that extends from three inches below the soil line to four inches above it—seven inches in all. The yellow and black moth deposits her eggs in the soil, which later become borers in the larval stage. If the hatching offspring cannot get into the tree, they starve to death. The masking tape will not bind the tree but will split as the trunk grows.

Pecans in the central states should be budded as soon as the bark on the seedling rootstock can be slipped. It is recommended practice to do this promptly, so the buds can be forced before midsummer. If held over, the dormant pecan buds in the refrigerator can be brought out now. Allow them to warm gradually at room temperature for 36 hours before beginning operations.

Fig trees in Zone Three through Zone Seven should be checked now for the presence of June bugs. The bugs can be handpicked if the trees are small, otherwise they should be shaken out of the branches. First spread a tarpaulin on the ground under the tree and be sure to destroy the pests before the fruit begins to ripen which is when they do the most damage.

From Zone Four southward, this is the last month for setting out new acerola bushes. Far-South residents should have at least one or a pair of these high-Vitamin C plants. Highest content is to be found in the Puerto Rican B-17, a tart variety; but you may find that the Florida Sweet Barbados cherry is better for picking-and-eating pleasure.

Newly-planted fruit trees or bushes should be watered once each week if the weather is dry, and given a thorough soaking then. But do not give them any extra or booster feedings this year. Instead, force the young root systems to stretch and reach out through and into the soil in search of food.

Blueberries should be watered and mulched now. Use sawdust only when a bush has been composted with manure for one full year. A mature bush requires a six-foot-wide circle of mulch. If the soil pH is greater than 5.0, apply pine needles, sphagnum moss or shredded oak leaves. But if the pH runs low, spread hay, straw, shredded corncobs or leaves.

Dewberries south of the Bluegrass Line will be ready for picking this month. Let them ripen fully for freezer and go quite soft. Cut all canes—new and old—to the ground as soon as the harvest is over, and spread compost or manure over the rows to encourage strong new growth. The new shoots can run along the ground until next spring when they should be tied up.

A good way to get rid of cooking and trimmed fats that can't go into the compost pile is to stuff the suet with mixed seeds for your bird feeding stations—this should also keep your home grounds insect-free. If you want to spoil or reward them, chunk-style peanut butter is highly esteemed by your feathered friends.

Under Glass

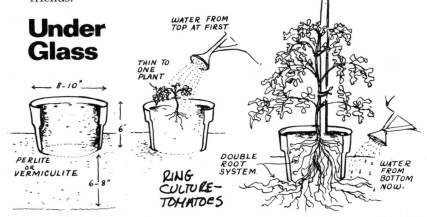

June is the ideal month to paint, clean up and generally renovate the greenhouse now that it is almost empty, and particularly if it has a wooden frame. Both inside and out can use a fresh coat of paint every two or three years, and to prevent peeling, the inside painting should be done now when the humidity is low. The outside should also be painted before the summer shades are put in place. To kill off fungus and algae, make an extra effort to get the empty benches sunned until they are thoroughly dry.

The greenhouse is by no means to be considered "closed for the season." Many plants, cuttings and seedlings will need continuing care. All the perennials and annuals—plus the vegetables—that were not set out last month should be planted outside early in June. If shading has not been placed, it should be done now.

If your greenhouse has no humidifier, extra wetting down will be called for in the areas under and between the benches, especially on the very dry and warm days. This watering will have to be continued throughout the rest of the summer.

Needless to say, good greenhousekeeping practices should be maintained, particularly because plant disease and insects multiply quickly in the warm, humid summer atmosphere. All dead or fallen foliage should be picked off plants, benches or paths. Feed the plants every two weeks—fish fertilizer diluted one tablespoon to a gallon of water can work wonders both for plants left in the greenhouse and those that have been set outdoors.

If the heating system has not been cleaned and inspected, it should be done at this time. If your greenhouse is made of wood, this is a fine time to apply a fresh coat of paint both on the outside and on the inside. Paint the outside early before the shading is applied and then do the inside before things heat up too much, preferably, when the humidity is low.

The hotbeds and cold frames should be open to the sun at this time. Remove the glass sash to a cool workbench where they can be reputtied and painted during the summer. Apply the putty to the scraped, cleaned and empty sash, and then put in the glass, pressing it down slowly, firmly and uniformly until the putty oozes out to fill the crack between the glass and frame. Then replace the fine metal wedges and paint over the joint to make everything waterproof and weathertight. Putty applied in this manner should not crack loose when water stands on the glass.

The houseplants that are getting their summer vacations outdoors should be watered regularly and generously—they are making their most active growth at this time, and can also use booster liquid fertilizer feedings. Manure "teas" are fine as is fish fertilizer mixed one tablespoon to a gallon of water.

Keep a careful eye, while you're at it, for infestation from garden pests such as mealy bugs and red spiders. The plants you have recently put out are still weak from their long winter stay indoors and, as a result, are particularly vulnerable.

As you put the plants out, take extra care in selecting sites for the different species—a full sun can be endured by very few house plants. Those which can stand more sun may be set in borders where they are reached by the sun in the morning and early afternoon but where they receive shade in the late afternoon. Among these are the astilbe, blue oxalis, bouvardia,

Christmas cherry, croton, hibiscus, jacobinia, oleander and peristrophe. Almost the only plants that enjoy the full, hot summer sun are the cacti, the succulents, geraniums and the coleus.

When shifting to their outdoor sites, sink the plants up to the heavy rims of their pots, leaving about one inch of the clay pot above the soil to protect against crawlers. While you're on the job, drop a trowelful of cinders below the pot to keep the pests from going through the drainage hole.

Just before sinking the pots in the garden, check their root systems. You don't have to haul the plants out, exposing their roots—just scratch the surface of the soil. If there are no roots crowding the top half-inch, repotting is not necessary. But it's a good idea to replace the top inch of soil with a rich compost before setting out in the garden.

The plants with a low light requirement that shrink from too much sun should be placed under trees or shrubs where only the low early morning rays can reach them. Set in such favored sites your azaleas, Star-of-Bethlehem, Christmas cactus, all ferns, plumbago, stephanotis, bird-of-paradise, star jasmine and winter flax. The bright-red fibrous-rooted begonias are very effective in front of evergreens. They should be removed from their pots and may be grown as border plants or planted thickly where they will make a dramatic mass effect.

Plants that are more sun-tolerant can be set in borders that get the early morning and afternoon sun but are shaded in the late afternoon. Among these are astilbe, Christmas cherry, hibiscus, croton, jacobinia, oleander and roses. About the only indoor plants that thrive in the full, hot summer sun are the cacti, the succulents, coleus and geraniums.

The fuchsia will do best on the porch when other shade is not available, while the Madagascar jasmine which requires deep shade should be grown on a trellis. The Jacobinia grows and blooms equally well in sun or shade, and a row in front of the evergreens or a low stone wall makes a highly effective border. Water freely and feed with liquid fish fertilizer every two weeks.

If you can find the time and place, it's a good practice to start tomatoes now in the greenhouse in time for next fall by following the ring-culture system. Prepare a six-to-eight-inch deep bed of gravel, perlite or vermiculite on the floor where drainage is good. Set tile or metal rings six inches deep and eight to ten inches wide—bottomless clay pots are ideal—on the vermiculite, and fill them with good loam enriched with organic fertilizers like bone meal, granite dust and cottonseed or soybean meal.

Plant the tomato seeds in the rings, and water them from the top until the roots have a chance to grow down to the perlite or vermiculite when they should be watered from below. According to those who have tried it, this method encourages the development of a double root system—one in the mice base and one in the clay pots which produces bumper crops in the late fall.

July
How Much Water Do Your Crops Need in July?

*And he gave it for his opinion, that whoever could make
two ears of corn, or two blades of grass, to grow upon a spot
of ground where only one grew before, would deserve better
of mankind, and do more essential service to his country than
the whole race of politicians put together.*

Voyage to Brobdingnag
Jonathan Swift

July's sudden cloudbursts will do little to help your thirsty
plants if you haven't mulched and the weather is very hot.
We're not talking about a prolonged drought which takes the
life out of the land, we're talking about topsoil that is baked
so dry by the sun that it puddles when a fugitive rain hits it.
There's no moisture bridge leading down through the soil to

your plants' root systems, and the water on top of the ground evaporates rapidly when the sun comes out again.

We'll get around to practical garden measures that, short of absolute disaster, will keep your garden soil moist all the way down to the root zone, and your plant stems turgid. What is turgor or turgidity? Plenty of moisture in the circulatory system of the plant so that it's round and full to the eye and pleasingly plump when gently palped. Writing in the 1955 *Agriculture Yearbook*, Leon Bernstein describes turgor as "the distended condition of the plant cells, necessary for continued plant growth." Without it, he wrote, a plant "cannot carry on photosynthesis effectively." When that happens, when the supply of carbon dioxide is cut off, both chemical changes within the plant growth stop. If the adverse trend continues, and the circulatory column of water that connects the roots to the leaves breaks, the siphon system no longer functions and the plant dies.

How much water do your row crops need in order to survive the rigors of a so-called temperate-climate summer? Here are some estimates, supplied by Victor R. Boswell and Larlowe D. Thorne, based on irrigation researches conducted by the Agricultural Experiment Station of California. They assume that "the root zone of the soil was well supplied with water at the time of planting." The varying amounts of water— rated in inches—that different vegetable crops need in order to flourish are as follows.

Winter lettuce and peas—6 inches; spinach—9 inches; cabbage, cauliflower, spring plantings of bush beans and lima beans—12 inches; onions (other than the late crop), pole beans, cucumbers, watermelons—15 inches; summer and fall lettuce, sweet corn, bush beans (summer plantings), beets, carrots, eggplant, peas, peppers, squash, muskmelon, sweet potatoes—18 inches; potatoes—20 to 30 inches; asparagus—20 inches; tomatoes (except in cool, coastal areas)—24 inches; celery—30.

Practically speaking, the small, backyard garden where many different vegetables are growing close together has to be handled on a different basis. You'll have to average out the amount of water you provide according to the weather, what's available in your community, and the amount of water the root zone can hold. Bear in mind that sandy soils can hold only one-fourth-inch of water per foot of depth, sandy loams hold three-fourths-inch per foot; fine sandy loams 1.25 inches; silt loams and clays hold between 2.5 and 3 inches.

That puts it squarely up to you and the watering can or hoseline. You can, of course, cut down on the above figures somewhat—or even more than that—by mulching conscientiously and intelligently as the benevolence of June gives way to the rigors of July. For many years now we have started out in the spring with almost bare ground which we covered gradually, starting with the between-row aisles and working closer and then closer to the plants.

Hay and straw are fine mulching materials if you can obtain a steady and sufficient supply. The same is true of wood chips or aged sawdust, providing you add a generous side-dressing of an organic nitrogen like blood or cottonseed meal. But if these materials are just not around when you need them, use whatever comes handy—many folks have used old carpeting between the rows. This year we're experimenting with a new biodegradable kraft paper mulch that comes in rolls, using it in the aisles and finishing off with hay around and between the plants. We'll have more to say about it later.

One more watering "trick." We're using perforated plastic hoses which go down the planting row *under the mulch*, putting water right where it will do the most good and where it will soak in without any loss from evaporation. Besides making the most effective use of your water— this method bypasses all danger from fungus infection of the leaves or foliage which is one of the big drawbacks of overhead spray irrigation systems.

Yes, it's July and your plants are growing faster now because the average temperatures range between 65 and 75 degrees. These figures apply to Zones One through Four—the rest of the country is about five degrees hotter. Your plants are working at top speed, sucking up water from the soil to fill the needs of every cell, while evaporation and transpiration are at a peak on the dry, clear and breezy days.

The old-timers had a phrase for it. "The birds are chirping for rain," they used to say when the weather went bone dry and stayed that way. But the birds are not alone—our gardens and their gardener-guardians may soon be asking for rain.

In the meantime—make sure you have plenty of mulch.

HERBS

The Vegetable Garden

If the early peas have already been harvested up in Zone Two country, the rows will be especially good now for fall cabbage, broccoli and celery. It's also time to sow winter carrots, fall salad greens and winter radishes.

Fall vegetables can also be planted early this month in the northern part of Zone Three. Among these are turnips, turnip greens, rutabagas, Chinese cabbage, fall salad greens, carrots and beets.

After planting, the rows should be shaded with burlap or cheesecloth pinned to racks or frames. If it's hard to keep even the shaded crops moist, start everything except the root crops indoors or in a lath house, transplanting the seedlings to the garden after hardening them off in the sun.

Best time to mulch is after a thunder shower, if you are so favored, when you will have fresh moisture to protect. The tiny weeds can be smothered; no need to pull them. But, whatever you use, draw the mulch up close to the stems of plants like peppers, eggplant, corn and tomatoes. The newspaper mulch will come in especially handy with the lettuce because it will save you extra-difficult washing later on.

Central states gardeners should be planting their fall vegetables this month—earlier in the month in the northern sectors, and later in the warmer. Chinese cabbage, carrots, fall salad greens, turnip greens and rutabagas may all be sown, and cabbage plants and cauliflower may also be set out.

This is the time to order seeds and make plans for the fall garden according to extension horticulturists stationed at Virginia Tech. They advise learning by heart the average fall frost date in your area, and then making your plantings far enough in advance so your crops will mature safely.

For example, most snap bean varieties take 54 days from planting to maturity. So, if your first frost date falls during the first week in October, you can plant snap beans as late as the first week in August. Sweet ripening corn takes about 66 days. In the early October frost areas, you can plant corn as late as the last week in July, and bring in a crop. And if the first frost is even later in your area—you can plant still later.

In most cases early-maturing varieties should be selected for the fall garden, coming on after your early summer crops have been harvested, and still available for picking before the ground freezes. Other excellent fall vegetables which should be planted about eight weeks before the frost date are beets, chard, kohlrabi, peas and turnips.

Toward the end of the summer, lettuce and spinach may be planted about six weeks before the frost date, and mustard and relish about two weeks later.

Cabbage, broccoli, cauliflower and kale should be seeded in early July. Prime Hybrid and Spartan Early are recommended broccoli varieties; little Rock and Globe are suggested cabbages while Snoball Imperial cauliflower is excellent for early July seeding.

Since the most serious problem associated with fall plantings is poor or irregular germination of seeds in dry soil, it's a good idea to wet the ground thoroughly the day before you plant. Then, after planting your seeds and covering with soil, spread a six-inch band of sawdust or shredded peat moss one-half-inch thick along the row to help conserve moisture and prevent soil crusting. If the weather stays dry, keep the rows moist with a sprinkling can or fine spray for about one week. Most of the seeds should germinate.

Further south, there's time to plant a fall crop of Irish potatoes now. Ask around, starting with your neighbors and ending with the county agent, to make sure you get a variety recommended for your area. Order seeds now for the fall-winter vegetable patch, and in August you'll be able to plant such winter-hardy crops as turnips, beets, spinach, winter carrots and the cabbages.

On the Pacific Coast, cabbages and Brussels sprouts may be set out now; fall carrots, turnips and kohlrabi may also be planted while another sowing of salad greens and bush beans can be made now.

Otherwise, produce should be plentiful in your garden at this time, and the only problem should be—what will you eat today? Zucchini and squash should be picked while their seeds are small—a dependable sign that they are tender. Kohlrabi should be picked while small—the size of golfballs— while beets and corn should be watched for peak goodness for the freezer as well as for the table. It's obviously good practice at this favored time to pay close attention to how the garden is coming on so you can pick your vegetables while they're at peak flavor and tenderness.

It's time to dry the herbs in your garden as they reach their prime. Work on a clear, hot day when you cut them, particularly if the forecaster promises you more of the same to come. The best flavor reportedly develops just before the blossoms open, although many herbs appear to be in good condition right up to the time when they dry out in the garden.

Select a hot attic or barn, and hang the herbs in a well-ventilated place where they will dry quickly but completely, and then store in glass jars with screw-on lids. Herb vinegar for next winter's salads should also be concocted now. Fill a bottle with tarragon, dill or your favorite mixture, and pour in wine vinegar to cover the herbs. Shake the bottle daily, strain off the vinegar in two weeks, and let settle before you use it.

You can freeze many without drying them, if you wish. Dip them briefly in boiling water, chop and freeze, either separately or in combinations that you favor when cooking. The separate herbs may be wrapped in twisted pieces of freezer paper, and then enclosed in labeled boxes.

Lath houses will pay for themselves out in the arid Southwest or on the southern coast of California. Build yours big enough to enclose the patio, and enjoy the lower temperatures that it brings. While you're about it, save a good spot—bed or border—for the summer salad greens. Black-seeded Simpson or Grand Rapids makes an attractive edging when alternated with the Ruby variety.

Melons can still be planted in the warm sections of the Pacific Coast. Melon vines in Zone Three should be getting fruit now. Protect the young fruit from beetles by putting shingles or thin boards under them before sugar begins to form. Fall cabbage, celery and broccoli plants should be set out before the end of the month, while seeds of Chinese cabbage can be planted in a shaded row.

Prepare a few portable cold frames for use later on. The double row kind—back to back—will allow you to do a little closer planting, and also take care of two rows at a time. Slant the windows high—about 40-45 degrees to grab all the sun you can and line the back of the inside frame with aluminum foil to throw the light back into the soil. You'll find that Chinese cabbage, escarole and endive can be picked from the garden until well after Thanksgiving if you put frames over them in the rows.

If you keep them, turn the chickens or ducks into the asparagus bed for a day or two after you finish cutting—they are death on asparagus beetles. If you live in the open country, pheasants may have already done the job for you. However, keep your maturing peas covered unless you have enough to feed both birds and humans alike.

It's wise to keep the compost pile moist during the hot weather. Also, aerate it or turn it, getting air into the center of the pile. If the weeds are starting to push up through the spring mulch, it's time to spread a few extra bales of hay where they will do the most good.

Best time for this chore is right after a summer shower when you have some fresh moisture to protect. The smallest weeds will be smothered by the hay—no need to pull them. If you have plenty of hay, work with "books" or two-inch layers which easily peel off the bale and make fine between-the-row mulch. For close protection, draw the straw right up to the stems of the tomatoes, peppers, eggplant and corn, using loose handfuls. When mulching next to lettuce, cover the row first with paper to save an extra-hard washing job later.

The Ornamental Garden

This is the season when bargains are being offered on leftovers in florist shops and garden supply stores.. Many of these can come in handy in odd corners of the borders and beds. Keep picking seedpods off all annuals to encourage bloom all summer.

If it has been dry, don't start watering your lawn unless you've got undisputed access to an unlimited water supply that will let you keep on watering the lawn all summer, regardless of the weather and local political ordinances.

The right way to water is when the soil is dry and then you should water deep—all the way down to the ends of the roots. To find out how far this is, dig down and come up with a spadeful of sod and then measure the roots. Then use an auger to bring up that much soil—six, eight, or more inches—to see if it is dry.

If it is, water until a second boring indicates that the water has percolated down to where it is needed. After successive testing you should know your lawn well enough to determine its water needs without more drilling.

Set the mower high to cut the grass at 2 1/2 to three inches —but keep at it!

Bermuda grass should be kept shorter than usual in humid weather to discourage fungus. Zoysia and also St. Augustine grass can be shaved for the same reason. But make sure your mower blades are keen and well-ground; a dull blade can damage the lawn by tearing the grass and bringing on the fungus you're trying to avoid.

If your area allows you ten or more weeks before the first fall frosts, you can still plant some of the short season annuals. A row of Shirley poppies in the iris bed will give you some pleasing late bloom, and if you let some of them run to seed you may have some volunteers next spring among the iris.

Zone Two residents should lift and divide Oriental poppies, mertensia and bleeding heart after their foliage dies back. While none of these normally requires attention, it may be time to move them to a freshly-fertilized bed if their bloom was not up to snuff. Madonna lilies which tend to crowd when left in one spot for five years may also be divided when they have finished blooming.

After July 15, gardeners in this area should stop pinching back chrysanthemums and give them a side-dressing of rotted manure, rich compost and bone meal to increase the size of the blossoms. Some gardeners may prefer an organic 2-5-2 mixture of two parts coffee grounds, one tankage, and one part bone meal.

Further south, roses should also be mulched with rich compost or rotted manure. Watch the grafted plants for suckers coming up out of the roots. They can frequently be spotted by their seven-part leaves on plants whose leaves only have five parts. Southeastern gardeners may do better with their finer-seeded annuals like petunias and lobelia, if they start them in pots or flats. A single five-inch seed pot will hold as many seedlings as you will want of either plant. Meanwhile, there is still time to plant marigolds, zinnias and torenia in the warmer sections.

Central staters put in the broad Zone Three area can perk up their summer rock gardens with French marigolds or gem petunias which can—with luck—be found blooming at bargain prices this month in the nurseries. If so, stock up on them generously. Otherwise there is still time to plant quick-blooming alyssum and candytuft.

At this time seed pods should be picked off all annuals that you'd like to keep with you. Otherwise they'll retire from the scene once their seed-producing chores are done. Sow fresh delphinium seeds as soon as they are available. It's a good idea to put your order in now, asking the seedman to make delivery as soon as they come in.

Again keep the faded blooms snipped off the floribundas to prolong flowering. Take great care not to remove the leaves with the flowers because the new clusters arise from the leaf axils. Ground corncobs make a good summer mulch for the roses but be sure to add cottonseed or soybean meal to maintain nitrogen levels in the soil.

In the drier parts of the Southwest, gardeners may want to encourage some favored growths with filtered sunlight from a lath house. Some plants which will appreciate and respond to the extra consideration include begonias, fuchsias, ferns and also primroses. If you've the time and space, add a few tall lilies and one or more gardenias for fragrance while, for a tropical touch, you might include a clump of bird-of-paradise and some cymbidium orchids.

Again, a lath house will pay its way during July and August in the more arid parts of the Southwest and also on the southern California coast. If you build one, be sure to make it large enough to take in your patio. You'll find inside temperatures average five degrees less, thanks to its semi-shade.

Zinnias will thrive in this area, provided they get plenty of water. If they are also given a side-dressing of cottonseed or blood meal, they will respond by producing some outstanding blooms. In addition, sow fast-growing annuals for fall bloom. Sweet alyssum, portulaca and California poppies are recommended for this season's planting.

The Orchard and Bush Fruits

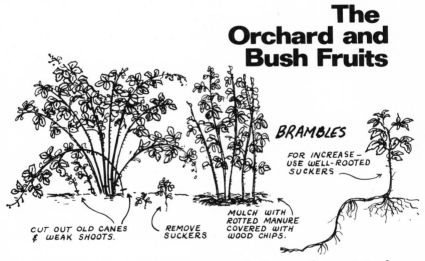

BRAMBLES

FOR INCREASE—
USE WELL-ROOTED
SUCKERS

CUT OUT OLD CANES
& WEAK SHOOTS.

REMOVE
SUCKERS

MULCH WITH
ROTTED MANURE
COVERED WITH
WOOD CHIPS.

It's time now to summer-prune all fruit trees that sustained winter-kill or damage that the tree has not been able to restore by itself. But go slowly and cautiously because summer pruning does not stimulate regrowth, and every cut you make now is a final one that cannot be corrected with time. If in doubt, and wherever possible, put off corrective pruning until next spring. But, while the ladder and cutters are out, go to work on the other trees that also sustained winter damage. The only trees that should be lopped and trimmed for shape are the espaliers.

As soon as the bramble harvest is finished, cut out all the old canes. This applies to the raspberries, blackberries and boysenberries. Also remove all the weak shoots, leaving only a half-dozen of the huskiest canes. All canes of the dewberries should be cut back to the ground. For the others, spread rotted manure or compost around the young shoots, and mulch well with wood chips after all straying, unwanted suckers have been dug up from the aisles. If you want to increase your stock, dig up as much root as possible when you're going after the suckers.

Watch your grapevines for mummies which should be removed immediately. If you're losing out to the wasps who somehow know before you when the grapes start to develop sugar, tie each cluster of grapes in a paper bag. In sugar production it is not necessary for the sunlight to reach the grapes because sugar is manufactured in the leaves and then transported to the grapes where it is stored.

If Concord grapes are afflicted with black rot which mummifies the fruit, practice strict sanitation. A round of careful daily inspection is needed, plus prompt removal and composting (be sure your pile is active!). Also keep an open eye for wild brambles near the garden that show wilted tops and have swellings in the canes. These can be the signs of borers that can next move into the garden itself, so it's wise practice to remove and destroy all infested wild canes.

During the hot months keep all newly-planted trees and shrubs well-watered. A good mulch of hay or straw will also help, especially if you keep adding to it. But do not use strawy manure during the first year (five years for young pear trees) because it's too rich. It's also a good idea to apply a coat of whitewash to the tender young trunks—it should prevent sunscald. Azaleas and camellias should be mulched lightly; they need plenty of air around their roots which are crowded just under the surface of the soil.

Keep an open eye for wild brambles near the garden that show wilted tops and have swellings in the canes. Borers may be present, and getting ready to move into your garden, so it's wise practice to remove and destroy all infested wild canes.

Pick up and compost all windfalls—your piles should be active and heating up well by now. This should be part of the daily operation—a good chore for the home-from-school junior gardener.

Papayas can be planted this month in Zone Seven in well-sheltered sites. Plant a pot-grown specimen if you can fine one.

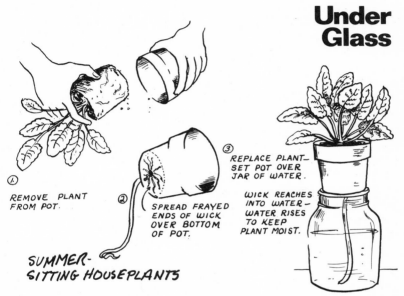

Under Glass

① REMOVE PLANT FROM POT.

② SPREAD FRAYED ENDS OF WICK OVER BOTTOM OF POT.

③ REPLACE PLANT— SET POT OVER JAR OF WATER.

WICK REACHES INTO WATER — WATER RISES TO KEEP PLANT MOIST.

SUMMER-SITTING HOUSEPLANTS

Presently start your cabbage and broccoli plants in flats or cold frames for planting out in Zones Four and south. They should go into the garden toward the end of August. The greenhouse glass should be whitewashed this month to cut down on the sun while the house itself is equipped with bamboo curtains or slatted matting—available at most garden centers, shopping centers or shopping center chain stores. This is a good garden investment which can come in handy in the planting rows, as well, when you want to pamper tender young plants.

Meanwhile, the family vacation can play havoc with the house plant schedule—unless you have a cooperative and understanding neighbor. But more likely, the plants will have to take their chances while you're away. Here are some of the things you can do to mitigate the rigors caused by your absence.

First, some of the plants can be left to shift for themselves under protective shrubbery, providing your climate is moderately rainy over the summer. But if you are not sure, move each plant to a somewhat more shady spot than it usually demands, and spread grass clippings over the soil in the pot.

You'll also find that the philodendrons and many of the summer indoor habitants will hibernate without harm while you're away if you slip a plastic bag over the plant including the foliage and pot. Water them well and leave in your coolest, dimmest room. Warning—don't follow this procedure for the succulents, the cacti or plants with spongy leaves.

While African violets, gloxinias and flame violets respond well to the water-wicking system, try out any self-watering system in advance, while you're at home and able to observe how it works and make the necessary adjustments. For each plant you need a wick—lamp or special plant wick (we've torn burlap and old sheets).

Working carefully and slowly, turn the plant out of the pot with as little damage as possible to the root ball, and spread the frayed end of the wick over the inside of the bottom of the pot, allowing the "stem" of the wick to hang down through the drain hole. Then refit the plant and root ball back into the pot firmly, making sure there is real contact between the wick and the soil. Next, stand each pot on top of a mason jar filled with water into which the wick is submerged. Water should gradually rise in the wick and up into the pot by capillary action to keep your plant watered while you're away. You can do the same thing, serving as many as six plants at a time, by using a watertight window planter so long as each plant has its own wick.

If you're staying home, this is the month to start cuttings from last year's house plants. This includes coleus, shrimp plant, wax begonias, fuchsia, aluminum plant, impatiens and geraniums, all of which can be started now for the winter window sill, thus saving many of them which would otherwise have to be discarded.

Make three- or four-inch cuttings from the tips of the growing stems, and remove all leaves except the new ones growing at the tip. Thrust the stems into three-inch pots filled with equal parts of sand, sphagnum moss and loam. Most of the above-mentioned plants will root easily in the mixture providing the pots are left in a warm shady place outdoors and are kept moist. But some, like the geraniums, prefer bottom heat for their cuttings.

It's time every few weeks to turn your house plants that are summering in the shrubbery. This serves a double purpose; it keeps the foliage symmetrical, and also prevents the plants from sending their roots deep into the garden soil, going through the drainage holes.

If you notice any trying to escape the pot, check to determine if their roots are too crowded. If they are, transfer to a larger pot. Or if the soil below the pot is more moist than the soil inside, remove some of the pebbled and broken bits of shard and replace them with sphagnum moss or peat.

All house plants should be fed liquid manure every two weeks during the summer. You can work with either the manure "tea" barrel or use liquid fish fertilizer mixed one tablespoon to a gallon of water. This applies equally to plants in the garden and to plants in the greenhouse, all of which are growing faster at this time than they did during the winter and need extra nourishment plus more water.

But try not to spoil your vacation with worry over your house plants when you do go away. A sympathetic neighbor with whom you have a firm two-way working arrangement is the best solution to the problem.

Finally, remember that it's sound policy to move each plant to a site that is shadier than its norm, and then spread grass clippings over the soil in each pot.

Even cacti and succulents set in their outside beds need watering at least twice a week. In the greenhouse, a humidifier can be a great help to the remaining plants, although sprinkling the paths and walks frequently should get the same results. In general, keep the greenhouse as cool as possible with shades and whitewash, and sprinkle the foliage of the house plants, feeding them liquid manure every two weeks.

August
In August, You Can't Lose

Songs Spring thought perfection,
Summer Criticizes:
What in May escaped detection,
August, past surprises,
Notes—and names each blunder.

Robert Browning

"In August, you just can't lose," the late Dorothy Franz once said. Her reasoning went as follows.

While August will be several degrees cooler than July— not enough to make much difference to us—our gardens will respond to these first hints of fall by maturing most of their crops. They've been officially told, so to speak. The abundance of the harvest will only rest in part upon temperature. The fullness of your freezer this winter will depend upon the amount of humidity, rainfall and sunlight your garden received over the seasons.

Rain may still be falling heavily on the eastern side of the Gulf Coast; New Mexico and Arizona are benefitting from what is for them a lot of rainfall, but the Plains States and the Pacific Coast may well be running dry—hot and dry. This fact not only makes Pacific Coast weather just right this month for curing all sorts of dried beans and fruits, but also makes the weather favor the big crop.

Up in Zones Three and Four—and they seem to take in 60 or 70 percent of the country—the July heat is badly punishing the leftovers from the spring crops. You're advised to pull up any beets and carrots that were planted in April "because their quality and vitamin content will be past peak." Incidentally, a hot August sun will delay the development of fall plantings of carrots in all areas. Carrots need a moderately cool, dry August; if your soil becomes wet and heavy this month, your fall carrots will tend to be short and thick, and will contain less vitamin A.

That same kind of weather—moderately cool and dry—will greatly help your potatoes, rutabagas and turnips. You'll get the most abundant spud yield from potatoes that stay in soil that's around 64 degrees throughout most of July and August. Too much starch is consumed in respiration at higher temperatures, and the tubers do not develop well. However, if the coolness is accompanied by too much moisture, you can get late blight which is caused by fungus growths. For the best results your potato vines should be well-mulched, cool, but not wet—that's the way to fill your potato bin.

Fall rutabagas and turnips can be damaged by a hot August which can cause them to put on poor growth. Rutabagas, in particular, suffer from the heat by developing long necks and poorly-shaped roots. Lettuce will not be heading in any part of the country this month, unless it is given special treatment. Also, hot days followed by hot nights can give it tipburn.

Thus far, August's score seems to be an adverse one; more loss and damage seem caused by the month's vagaries than benefits received. But events have a way of evening out in nature although the blossoms of several types of plants can be damaged and made barren, sometimes for weeks at a time. Snap beans, for example, can be delayed in this manner. But the August temperatures are usually perfect for tomatoes because they flourish in the 70- to 75-degree averages.

If, however, the average goes above 80 and is accompanied

by low humidity, the flowers can be damaged before the fruit sets. The peppers can take a little more heat, but when the daily maximum stays above 90 degrees for a protracted period, it interferes with fruit setting. When peppers set at between 80 and 90 degrees, the fruits may assume abnormal shapes.

And now for the happier aspects of the month. Late varieties of corn need high temperatures now to make good growth, while ample rainfall until the middle of August will also help boost yields. But watch it if any of your corn is reaching maturity in hot weather! Peak quality lasts only one or two days in hot weather; unless you like your corn tough, you have to catch it "at almost the exquisite moment for the freezer."

Again, cheer up. High temperatures in August are good also for sweet potatoes—an average of 75 degrees will give you the best crop. But then, think it over. Heat of this kind "may spell the end of the cucumber vines."

So, Dorothy Franz concluded, "if August is hot, we'll have lots of sweets, late corn and melons—the heat-lovingest crop of all. If it is cool, our lettuce, potatoes and fall crops will prosper. And if it's just average, our tomatoes and peppers will do well."

And that's why you "just can't lose" in August.

The Vegetable Garden

If you plan to save your own seed, mark the tomato plant that bore the earliest fruit. In most zones, early fruiting is the most desirable trait you can develop in your own tomato strains.

Pest control will be much easier in next year's garden if you pull and shred each cornstalk, bush squash plant, bean and cucumber vine promptly when it is through bearing. After shredding, turn the residues into the compost pile immediately in order to kill off the eggs of such predators as the Mexican bean beetle and squash bug.

However, some gardeners advise us that allowing the pole

limas, green or wax beans to mature and dry on the vines is good practice. According to them you don't know what baked beans can taste like until you cook up a batch of your own organically-grown beans.

The pods should be left hanging until after the first frosts unless they show a tendency to shatter. That's the time to shell and store them in the freezer (space permitting) until it's time for the midwinter pots of baked beans. So, with beans, you've got a choice—pest control or tasty winter beans. May be a good idea to let the season decide for you—a pest-free year should be a safe one for experimentation.

Garlic, onions and shallots should be braided and stored now in a handy side or backroom that's cool and shaded. The tops should be thoroughly dried before braiding, and weave a length of heavy cord into the braid for extra strength. Don't include any thick-neck onions in the braids because they will not keep.

Pull up and compost the cornstalks as you strip them. The latest ears will have fewer earworms and smut when the early stalks are removed promptly from the garden.

If you disbud the vines toward the end of the season, the late tomatoes will be larger and better. Six weeks before the first fall frost in your area, start removing the growing tips of each branch and, from that time on, nip out all blossoms— it takes more than six weeks for a blossom to mature. Doing this conserves the plant's energy for the developing fruit because it prevents the growth of marble-sized tomatoes that would be caught by the frost and never used.

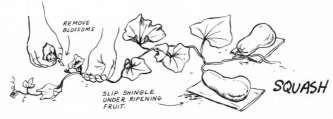

Mulch should be checked in all warm areas and renewed where it is working thin. This applies especially to crops that will bear in the fall. From now, remove new blossoms from melon and winter squash. As with the tomatoes noted above, only the blossoms already set will be able to develop mature fruit after the first of the month. Check fruits now where they rest on the ground. If the bugs have been busy, slip a shingle or flattened tin can under each melon or squash.

Sow winter rye or ryegrass in the patches vacated by early crops for turning under next spring.

Central states' gardeners can dig their potatoes now and store them as soon as the tops die. Or, they can be left in the ground until just before the first frost—whichever seems better to you. Unless you have a very fine root cellar, the ground is an excellent storage place.

White potatoes can be planted at this time in the Southwest for a fall crop. If you want good-sized spuds, be prepared to irrigate. Now you can also set out celery, collards and turnips. It's also time to give a side-dressing of cottonseed or blood meal mixed with bone meal to the eggplant, okra, peppers and pimentos. If it's easier, you can feed them manure water after irrigating.

Watch ripening tomatoes for the first signs of blossom endrot. If you find any, increase the watering, and keep in mind that tomato roots stretch out as much as two or three feet in all directions. It's also good to check if the plants need an extra layer of fresh mulch.

Late tomato plants should be set out this month in the warmer zones. Soak the soil deeply before setting out the plants, and give each one a cupful of manure water when you plant it. Be sure to allow no more than one foot of the plant to extend over the top of the soil—even where the plant is large—and remember to set the plants two inches lower than they were in the plant bed.

The winter vegetables should be sown this month in all gardens from Zone Two southward. In the coldest areas plant only the vegetables that will mature before the heavy freezes arrive, plus those crops that can stand freezing without damage. This includes carrots, field salad (available from Joseph Harris, Rochester, New York, and Burnett Bros., 92 Chambers Street, New York, New York), leeks and parsnip. And there is still time, in most of Zone Two, to plant escarole, Chinese cabbage, fall radishes, endive and turnips.

In Zones Three and Four start lettuce in cold frames or beds that can be covered when the first frosts arrive. In Zone Five south, plant bush squash and beans, kale, black-eyed peas, beets, chard, collards, Chinese cabbage, carrots, sweet corn and turnips. In Zones Six and Seven, plant cabbage, cauliflower and celery seed.

Where frost is expected in the higher elevations in late October or November, plant snap beans, broccoli, Brussels sprouts, cabbage, carrots, cauliflower, collards, sweet corn, cucumbers, endive, head lettuce, parsley, New Zealand spinach and turnips.

If you're feeding the vegetable patch extra water, it's extremely likely that the compost piles are also drying out. Give them a good drenching, and then cover them with straw, a tarpaulin or soil. Bacterial action is at its peak when the pile is moist and well-aerated. Since you will need all the compost you can make for the fall, be sure to start an extra pile now, especially if you will plant trees and shrubs in the autumn.

Otherwise, a thick layer of straw over the top of the heap is a good way to shade it from the sun. Another moisture saver —provided you have had rain—is a shallow well left in the center of the pile to gather any rain that falls and also to prevent runoff.

Cabbages should be watched for harlequin bugs—red and black—that suck the plant dry and leave it limp. Hand-picking, though time-consuming, seems the best way to overcome these pests; badly infested plants should be pulled up and destroyed.

The Ornamental Garden

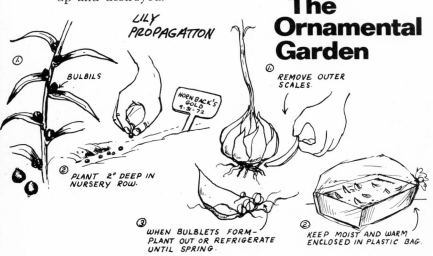

LILY PROPAGATION

① BULBILS

② PLANT 2" DEEP IN NURSERY ROW.

③ WHEN BULBLETS FORM— PLANT OUT OR REFRIGERATE UNTIL SPRING.

HORN BACK'S GOLD 4-31-72

① REMOVE OUTER SCALES.

② KEEP MOIST AND WARM ENCLOSED IN PLASTIC BAG.

How are your August perennials? Are there any in bloom now? If not, plan to put in some of these in time for next year:

Aconitum uncinatum, coreopsis, helenium, mallow, plantain lily, speciosum and L. henrix, liatris and rudbeckia.

It's time for northern gardeners to take cuttings from their prize roses for rooting outdoors. Best to work in advance, preparing a shady bed of peat mixed with sand. Then when your nippers have an extra-keen, smooth edge, take your cuttings and insert them, watering them well, and covering each with a glass jar which will not be removed until next spring. While you're busy around the roses, watch out for sucker growths at, or just below, the bases of the grafted hybrids. Remove any that you find to prevent reversion to the rootstock parentage.

New England and Pacific Coast gardeners should disbud and feed their chrysanthemums and dahlias at this time for extra-large blooms. For exhibitions, plants should be side-dressed with cottonseed or blood meal and given liquid fish fertilizer every three weeks.

August is a good month for remodeling and working over the rock garden. Stuff trowelfuls of compost under stones that shelter weed roots, lifting the rocks to do so, and then carefully replacing them. Divide the spring-flowering plants that are over-crowded, and thin the more competitive growths, planting the excess trimmings on the edges of your wild areas.

Central staters in the expansive Zone Three area who have experienced a dry summer should water the heaths, roses, flower borders and newly-planted ornamentals. Be generous when watering to make sure that the water gets down to the deepest roots.

This is the month in the Deep South to order your spring-flowering bulbs both for winter forcing and for next year's borders. If you are in Zones Six and Seven, refrigerate the bulbs on arrival and plant them in November or December after they have been in the refrigerator for three months. The long-stemmed Darwins or Breeders are recommended for the best results.

Do not plan on growing flowers from the same bulbs next year. Unless your region experiences regular, periodic, prolonged frost and chilling over the winter, you must grow your tulips strictly as if they were annuals.

Bulbs which may now be set out in the Southwest include

Madonna lily and iris. Columbine and gaillardia seed may be planted for next year's perennial borders, while snapdragons, calendula, pansies and violas can be planted for winter bloom this year. Hardy amaryllis should presently be set out by burying the entire bulb in the hottest areas up to the neck. Best foods for cacti are wood ashes, bone meal and well-rotted cow manure.

Annuals for late fall- or winter-flowering should be started now. And you may begin your perennials for next summer, including baby's breath, coreopsis, gaillardia and valerian. In the warmer areas, place calendula in sheltered spots.

Gardeners further north who want a variety of bloom next spring should finish planting their basic perennials. Biennials should include campanula, forget-me-nots, foxglove, pansies, Siberian wallflower and verbascum. These may be sown directly in the border or in the cold frame. Most biennials will self-sow once they are established in the garden.

Now's the time to give peonies a side-dressing of cottonseed meal, bone meal and granite dust. If you're near the ocean try mulching your peonies with seaweed—it's excellent.

In the central states, peony growers should also side-dress their plants with a complete and balanced fertilizer. Dahlias will bear extra-large exhibition blooms when they are given a nitrogen-rich feeding of cottonseed or blood meal. And, to be sure of very large blooms, disbud rigorously. This also applies to chrysanthemums which should be fed liquid manure or fish fertilizers.

Further west, gardeners should be finished planting perennial and biennial seeds in lathhouse nursery beds. Winter annuals may be started in the milder areas, and July seedlings should be ready for planting before they become too leggy.

Larkspur seed should be refrigerated now for spring bloom. Store in the icebox until a few 40-to-45-degree days arrive, and then plant outside. Don't forget that larkspur will not germinate in warm weather.

With some help from the nursery lilies may be propagated at this time. Bulbils in the leaf axils of tiger lilies, Lilium sargentiae, L. sulfureum and some of the new hybrids will soon be ripe. Remove them before they fall, and plant them like seeds in flats or nursery rows.

The lilies that do not produce bulbils can also be propagated as soon as they have finished blooming. Just lift the largest bulb, and remove the outer layer or two of scales, breaking them off close to the base. Handle the scales like bulbils, and next year they'll be ready for transplanting six inches apart in nursery rows. In two to three years they will reach blooming size. Be sure to replant the mother bulbs after removing the scales.

The soil under the rhododendrons and azaleas should be kept well-watered while the weather is hot, then allowed to dry somewhat as the autumn comes on. While the soil should never be completely dry, the summer's growth will harden more surely before the cold weather arrives if you hold back on the water in the autumn.

Leggy rhododendrons will benefit from summer pruning. If necessary, cut back to a rosette of leaves, and try your hand at disbudding. While no absolute rule can be given, a little judicious and observant experimenting can give you fewer but more magnificent blooms which you may prefer to clusters of mediocrities. Some growers advise that varieties with large flower trusses should be allowed to produce only one bud to a square foot of plant surface. Moreover varieties that tend to thrust both foliage and flowers straight up can be induced to spread out laterally when disbudded.

A hot, damp August can lead to fungus attacks in the beds and borders. The most susceptible areas include the chrysanthemums, crape myrtle, roses, verbena and zinnias. The mildews and molds are best discouraged by thinning out growths that are too thick, thus getting air into the plant clusters.

Red spider infestations can be fought with summer spraying of the affected foliage. Morning and late afternoon are the best times—if possible, you should avoid wetting foliage under the hot midday sun.

Start to prepare the soil for fall-seeded lawns. Grass that is started in September or October has the best chance to successfully hold its own with local weeds. When you dig and grade the lawn this month, build in as much humus as you can. Rock phosphate is very important. Apply it 100 pounds to each 1,000 square feet. In severe cases you may have to rotary-till the mixture, and then rake and roll for grade and smoothness. Finally, when you seed, be sure to cover with scattered straw. In the case of steep banks or slopes, peg down wetted burlap.

The Orchard and Bush Fruits

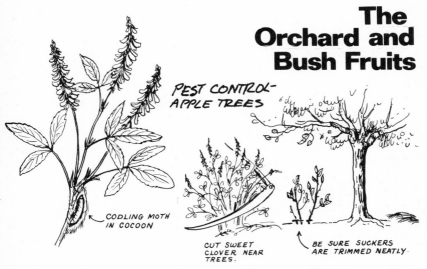

PEST CONTROL- APPLE TREES

CODLING MOTH IN COCOON

CUT SWEET CLOVER NEAR TREES.

BE SURE SUCKERS ARE TRIMMED NEATLY

As soon as their harvest is finished, prune old canes from the loganberries, boysenberries and youngberries. Be sure to leave no nesting places for pests—cut each cane level with the ground. The only bushes whose old canes should be left undisturbed are the Evergreen and Himalaya blackberries—their canes are perennial and will bear again next year. Prune the new canes to leave only three or four to each plant.

It's time, further North and along the West Coast, to give fruit trees their summer pruning. Cut out all water spouts, broken wood and poorly-colored fruit which is generally caused by insufficient exposure to the sun. Remember, when pruning next year, to open up the center of the tree to correct this condition. Also, make only the absolutely necessary cuts at this time because summer pruning reduces the tree's production—the wood doesn't grow back as it does with spring pruning.

Check the ground under the trees while you're cleaning up. If you kept a thick mulch most or all of the season, it might help avoid a pest infestation to rake away the old mulch, compost it, and apply fresh.

While they seldom attack healthy trees, bark beetles should be checked out in your apple and cherry trees. The pests are also called shot-hole borers because they make small holes in the branches. You can usually detect these holes by looking for a small trickle of sap below them. Remove and destroy the afflicted branches and mark the tree for an extra dose of fertilizer in the spring.

The wild and weedy areas around your fruit plantings should be investigated for the presence of sweet clover and native bramble bushes. Codling moth cocoons are sometimes found in the sweet clover stems, spun lengthwise in cottony masses, while the swollen canes of the wild bramble growths may indicate the presence of borers. Such canes should be destroyed, and the sweet clover should be mowed.

As soon as the harvest is finished, start a clean-up of each tree by removing all mummified fruits, including those on the ground. By now your compost piles should be at peak performance—get your fruits close to the center of active piles, spread in thin layers. Once again, at the Experimental Farm, John Keck builds very wide (six or more feet), flat, three-feet-high piles of leaves and wood chips. He deposits the fruits in the center of the pile where they compost safely without spreading disease. Finally, check the ground under the trees while you're cleaning. If you kept a thick mulch most or all of the season, you can probably avoid a pest infestation by raking away the old mulch, composting it and applying a fresh mulch.

Be sure to prop, brace, and otherwise secure, heavily-laden branches in hurricane- and tornado-prone areas before the storm season arrives. These precautions particularly apply to the states just north of the Gulf of Mexico. If your citrus trees suffered injury last winter, this is the time to prune out all branches which have shown no signs of recovery. While you're at it, look for the new shoots which tangle with or interfere with old branches, and prune them or direct them to grow to the outside of the tree.

Sweet clover should be cut back near apple trees because codling moths like to spin their cocoons along its sterns. When mowing, watch out for fruit tree suckers. If you leave trees with ragged stumps, they provide excellent propagating and hibernating spots for many kinds of insects.

Under Glass

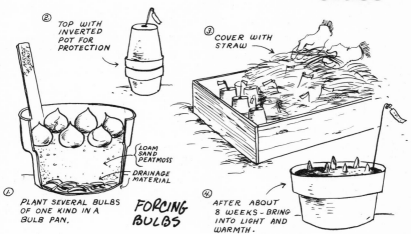

② TOP WITH INVERTED POT FOR PROTECTION

③ COVER WITH STRAW

{ LOAM
  SAND
  PEATMOSS

DRAINAGE MATERIAL

① PLANT SEVERAL BULBS OF ONE KIND IN A BULB PAN.

FORCING BULBS

④ AFTER ABOUT 8 WEEKS - BRING INTO LIGHT AND WARMTH.

Flowers that may be started in August in the greenhouse include calendula, clarkia, fairy primrose, schizanthus and the cyclamen Persica which blooms from seed in about five months. Be sure to use only the varieties of snapdragon that are winter-blooming—the summer varieties require longer days for flowering.

The fall vegetables that were started earlier under glass should be shifted now to the garden rows and patches. Give each one a cup of manure water or liquid fish fertilizer when you put them out, and mulch well. If you're short of material, remember to run your old newspapers through the shredder or pulp them with water.

If the sun is especially hot in your area, protect the tender young plants with half-bushel baskets for the first few days just as you did in the spring. Root crops that can be planted right in the ground include radishes, carrots and beets. Kale, Swiss chard and scallions will pay later for the little room they take up now.

The winter crops that can be started now include lettuce and tomatoes. Take cuttings or slips from your garden tomato plants and root them in open-bottom tubs. Fireball, Marglobe, Rutgers and the pear-shaped Italian San Marzono are ideal for this.

Remember that you're forcing things somewhat; be prepared to do some hand-pollinating with a camel's hair brush. Also, keep night heat between 60 and 65 degrees and supply extra light—incandescent as well as fluorescent to get the benefits of the red side of the spectrum.

If you have an electric-heated hotbed—the G.E. cable unit complete with soil thermostat, is good for a six-by-six bed and costs about $15—now is the time to prepare it with plenty of your best screened compost for your fall and winter supply of Bibb lettuce. Start the Bibb in rows spaced one foot apart, and interplant between the rows with Black-Seeded Simpson which can be taken up and used at the table while it is still too small to compete with the Bibb.

August is a good time to dress up the tired window boxes by removing the now-exhausted annuals and replacing them with low, bushy varieties of chrysanthemums. Azalea mums that are budding at this time are good for this project. While you're at the window areas, make some cuttings of fuchsias, geraniums and English ivy for the winter windowsills.

As soon as the bulbs for forcing arrive, pot them and then prepare a cold frame for them. Pots of daffodils, hyacinth, narcissus and tulips should be plainly labeled before being sunk in a bed of ashes in the frames and then covered with a thick layer of straw. Do not close the frames because the bulbs need moisture while they are making roots.

Start pots of calla lilies and freesias in the greenhouse for winter bloom. Give them a cool place under the bench, and keep them slightly moist until growth begins. To obtain a succession of freesias, keep adding a few more plants every three or four weeks.

Strawflowers and other specimens may be cut now to dry for winter arrangements. On your daily stroll, keep an open eye for attractive seedpods, grasses and cattails so you will have time to pick them before they shatter. Most dried material can be prepared just by hanging it upside down in an airy attic.

Some flowers generally not considered winter bouquet material, may also be dried when given a little extra care. Among these are bells of Ireland, some roses, asters, dahlias, nigella, lantana, rose-of-Sharon, tithonia and zinnias. All of these can be preserved if the flower heads are buried in fine, dry sand for four or five days. Be sure that the sand is completely dry and that you have enough of it to do a thorough job of burying your specimens.

Sift the sand over and around each flower, working slowly and carefully so you don't crumple the petals. At the end of the drying period, carefully dig out the flowers and store them in boxes until winter.

Check the house plants that are vacationing outdoors just once more. Lift each pot to make sure that the roots are not growing through the drainage hole. If they are, the plant has made too-rapid growth, is pot-bound, and needs a larger container, or else, the drainage is too free. In the latter case, change the potting mixture so it contains more humus and less sand.

Continue to feed tubbed oleanders every two weeks as long as they bloom. Allow flower stalks to fall off by themselves, but remove all faded blossoms. Pinch back the new shoots that hide the flowers. If the weather has been dry, tubbed acacias should be watered generously, while daphne, azaleas and camellias should be kept moist at all times. Allow allamandas to dry off gradually as dormancy approaches.

September
Four Garden Projects for September

Not leaves only, but all garden wastes and all plant residues should be returned to the soil. Then and only then will your garden equal and even surpass the pictures in the seed catalogs...

William H. Eyster, Ph.D.

September is the "lookout" month of the garden, according to Dr. William Eyster. From its vantage point, he observed, you should be able to "properly evaluate the worth of your garden."

Well, how *have* crops been? Have January's plans come to fruition in September? Will the freezer fill up this fall and earn its keep, or will the pickings be lean? If so, it's too late to blame things on the weather, our possible lack of horticultural skill and expertise—and just plain bad luck. Let's start thinking about next year and how we can garden better.

Here are four garden projects that can be started this month and completed the next and have helped us over the rough spots and actually made us garden better. They are: 1—Building movable cold frames for earlier plantings and second cropping; 2—Making wire racks of frames to protect tender young plants and also support them; 3—Starting a new herb bed, preferably near the kitchen; 4—Gathering and using leaves wholesale in the garden.

We first saw these portable cold frames up at Stephen Chelminski's homestead in West Redding, Connecticut, just across the road from Ruth Stout's place. They're 16 feet long and wide enough at the bottom to fit around a row comfortably. The covers are slanted or tapered 18 inches from back to front to admit as much sunlight as possible and are hinged to stay upright without tipping.

Two men can carry one frame to any part of the garden where it's needed. If you're going to build one or two such frames, plan them carefully in advance to fit your growing rows. It's also good to run your rows from east to west so they can benefit from a southern exposure. Making row-long wire racks or frames, also movable, is quite easy and simple. Two of you can put together a 30-foot-long triangular protective rack in about as many minutes. Cost is not low, about $10 for a 30-foot frame made of 14-gauge, four-foot-wide wire. But we used our set of frames for many years and found that they pay for themselves in late crops and also rescued crops of lettuce, peas, spinach and beans.

The wire comes in rolls, three or four feet wide. A four-foot roll with two-foot sides stands 18 inches high; a three-foot roll is 15 inches high. When measuring off the length of wire you need, add six feet to allow for end flaps, plus clearance. Fold the length of the wire down its middle using a heavy straight plank for a guide. Then make a careful, accurate, and even fold with a 90-degree angle. Cut down the center fold at each end to make flaps and fold them over and under to seal off the end. Bend the bottom over to make an even edge that will sit on the ground and keep small predators like rabbits on the outside.

Such racks have many uses. Here are four: 1—Keeping wild-life away; 2—Protecting plants from early and late frosts, also from the midsummer sun by draping light cloth over the rack; 3—Training young plants by using the frames as racks or scaffolds; 4—Keeping leaves in place where they protect your planting rows all winter.

When we made a new herb bed we located it on the top of a grassy slope that was infested by stoloniferous crabgrass which made for complications. How to get the stuff out permanently? But—no matter. The new four-by-20 bed got the sun from the crack of dawn to late in the day, was sheltered from the north by the huge bank barn, and faced due south. What if its soil was filled with crisp, white, never-ending crabgrass roots? Here's how we solved the problem.

We collected a great supply of old newspapers, magazines, chunks of linoleum, bits of carpeting and rugs, some tired old plywood, plus all the other flat and opaque material we could scrape up. We set this collection flat down on the strip in overlapping layers with about a one-foot overhang all around. Then we topped this none-too-handsome junkpile off with rocks and stones and let it go to work keeping the light and air away from the offending grass.

P.S.—it worked. Six weeks later every blade and root of grass beneath our odd blanket was dead and we were ready for our soil-enrichment program. Since we had started the project in September, the sixth week brought us into the middle of October when plenty of leaves were available. Into the shredder they went, later to be turned under by the rotary tiller which mixed the dead sod into the now-friable soil. Later we added rock fertilizers, ground limestone, wood ashes and bone meal and compost. We coated the entire area with coffee grounds and found it teeming with earthworms in the spring when we planted our first lettuce, shallots, garlic and parsley.

As for the leaves, it's just about time to start studying local curving and climbing roads to see where the wind tends to deposit the trees' bounty in knee-high heaps and windrows. You'll save yourself a lot of extra raking and gathering by knowing just where to go when the leaves begin to eddy down and collect at the sides of the road or beside a grassy bank.

If you bring along a tarpaulin, a grass rake and broom, two of you can fill the average station wagon—back to front, top to bottom—in about 20 minutes. Three such trips can fill a good-sized wire enclosure which stores your leaves until you're ready to use them.

But it's out in the vegetable patch that the leaves should really be "stored"—and used. Deposit them alongside next year's planting rows and then follow up with the shredder straddling the actual row. Fill up the hopper and shred right over the row, depositing on it a mellow aggregate that will readily convert into a soil-conditioning humus.

Later, it's time to follow up with the rotary tiller, turning the leaves under, and adding rock minerals. You can add some form of nitrogen, but it might be thriftier to wait until next spring to avoid loss from leaching. Finally cover the rows with still more leaves, this time unshredded, holding them in place with the row-long wire cages that you made just for this— and other—garden occasions.

And these are the four projects that, started this September, will help next year's garden "equal and even surpass the pictures in the seed catalogs."

The Vegetable Garden

Zone One and Two gardeners should keep a weather-eye open for unseasonably early frosts, and keep a supply handy of emergency cover material to protect tomatoes and other tender plants from the first frosts. If they can get through the first chilly night without harm, they should be expected to last a couple of extra weeks before the weather really turns cold. In Pennsylvania we build protective frames around the tomato rows using bales of hay and cover them at night with storm windows. We found this gives the plants real protection and permits us to "extend" the season about two weeks.

Otherwise, temporary cold frames should be made up or repaired throughout the combined areas, ready to protect the tender crops at the first frost and the hardy ones later on when the real freezes arrive. This is recommended for late-planted endive, celery, Brussels sprouts, Chinese cabbage and cauliflower, where early freezes are the rule.

If wet, cold soil is your problem in the spring, plan now to avoid it by fall fertilization and turning of the earth. This will enable you to get the earliest-possible start next year with your peas, lettuce, onions and radishes. After turning under your compost and nutrients, cover the soil with straw or hay that can easily be removed in the spring so the soil can warm up as fast as possible. We've successfully planted green peas in such pre-prepared rows during late February thaws that exposed the soil. While you're about it, turn under fresh manure for the first plantings of peas, onions, carrots, beets, and lettuce.

Otherwise, where the ground is less difficult, it's time to start winter cover crops or sheet-composting operations in all areas where the vegetable garden will lie fallow for the next few months. A buckwheat cover can be sown after the first frost in Zones Two and Three in the Northeast at the rate of two bushels to the acre—recommended practice for building up acid soils.

Sow cowhorn turnips two pounds to the acre if you're fighting hardpan conditions. After they are killed by the cold, the long roots will break down, leaving long drainage channels ranging through the subsoil.

Cover crops that should be sown at this time include fenugreek sown 35 to 40 pounds to the acre in Zone Five, and unhulled clover seed sown three to six bushels to the acre in Zones Four through Seven.

It's good practice, too, to collect all available organic materials for sheet composting over the winter. The lumber yard is still turning out sawdust while the dairies, pony rides and egg-raising farms are still in business.

As fast as the garden rows empty, cover them with layers of materials that will break down over the winter so that the bed or patch can be turned under in the spring. Shredded leaves, spoiled hay, fresh manure, ground corncobs, beans and peanut shells all make fine cover. Also, add such slow-working soil-conditioners as granite dust and ground bone meal so they'll be available for spring growing.

Further south, in Zones Three and Four, plantings may still be made of late turnips, while parsley and lettuce may also be planted now for spring use. Mustard, spinach and carrots may be planted among the fruit trees, so they may be turned under in the spring for an extra supply of humus.

In the warmer parts of Zones Four through Seven, this is the month to start succession plantings of beets, carrots, kale, lettuce and turnips. In the coastal Northwest, garlic, onions and asparagus may be planted now for a brief cutting in the spring. In Zones Six and Seven in the Southeast, garden peas, beans and most of the other popular vegetables with the exception of corn, okra and melons, may be planted. Gardeners in the southwest parts of Zone Six should make certain they irrigate thoroughly before setting out vegetables or planting seed. Bush beans, planted there now, will be ready for the Thanksgiving dinner.

For Alabama gardeners, September 20 is the date for planting kohlrabi, mustard, radish and turnip seed. The same sowing date applies to central Florida residents who want to plant snap beans, field peas, okra, cucumbers and mustard.

In the central states winter pumpkins, squash and gourds may be picked with two-inch stems if they are ready. Store the pumpkins and squash at about 60 degrees, and dry the gourds indoors. Lift and pot young parsley plants for indoor use. In the colder areas rosemary and lavendar may be wintered in cold frames or potted. Chives should be potted and stored under straw in a cold frame until they have been chilled. When they are chilled, bring them in to be forced as you would force tulips.

Leave a two-inch stem on to prevent rot when you pick the mature gourds and dry them indoors. If you think it safe, leave them on the vines until the seeds rattle when shaken. Since pumpkins and winter squash will spoil indoors if the temperature is too low, be sure to store them at or near 60 degrees.

Having trouble gathering mulch for your Zone Three vegetables? You might try this plan originally devised by John Krill of North Lima, Ohio. Here's how it works. Start sprouting oat seed now, keeping it moist and warm until shoots are about two inches long—which is long enough to discourage marauding crows.

If sprouting is started in the middle of the month, shoots should be long enough in about two weeks for the next step which is to scatter the sprouted seeds over the top of the existing mulch. If done at just the right time, this seed will provide a growth that will be cut down by frost before it makes seed and thus will provide cover for the winter and spring vegetable patch.

Out in the warmer parts of the Pacific Coast, there is still time to plant winter radishes, turnips and fall salad greens in the emptied vegetable rows. Is municipal sludge available in your area? You can prevent erosion and surface wear by covering the rest of the garden area with organic, humus-creating materials—manures and leaves included.

As is customary at this time, it's good practice to get ready to cover the ground over the winter—except in desert areas. Work with what is abundant locally like leaves and sludge, plus the crop residues from your own garden. Be prepared next spring to haul everything off to one side to give the soil a chance to warm up as quickly and deeply as possible. This practice is especially recommended for those areas where the spring comes on late and cold.

The Ornamental Garden

September is the month to plant hardy perennials such as bleeding heart, lily of the valley and most rock garden plants and all members of the narcissus family including the crocuses, snowdrops, scillas and other small bulbs. Depth of planting should be three times the height of the bulb while the bulbous irises and peonies should not be set more than two inches down. When planting, be generous with bone meal and compost. Planting in such a manner should make crops well-established before winter arrives.

In Zones One and Two seed for English daisies, forget-me-nots and pansies can still be planted in cold frames. In Zones Four and Five, they can be started outdoors. Zone Six gardeners in the Southwest can plant such winter annuals as sweet alyssum, stock, calendula, cineraria, snapdragons, petunias, Iceland poppies, lobelia and larkspur.

In the Southeast, in Zones Six and Seven, beds should be prepared now for next month's planting of annuals. The early-flowering sweet peas may be planted now, also next year's perennials. Dig caladium bulbs when their foliage dies back, dry them thoroughly, and store in vermiculite in a cool but not freezing cellar.

It's time now to overhaul the perennial beds in Zone Two and Three gardens. The crowded spring-bloomers such as lily of the valley, primroses, peonies, daylilies, coral bells and bleeding heart should all be lifted and divided now. Dig rock fertilizers into each hole and be generous with the peat moss when the beds appear to lack humus. Try not to bury your row markers as you go—you'll be grateful to yourself for your thoughtfulness next spring.

② HANG BY TOPS UNTIL DRY.

GLADIOLA

① LIFT CORMS WHEN FOLIAGE YELLOWS.

When their leaves turn yellow, lift the gladiolus corms, hanging them by their tops until the leaves dry and may be separated easily from the bulbs. Then store the corms in a well-ventilated root cellar that is cool but not freezing throughout the winter. If you pack them in fresh wood chips or shavings, they will dry out less and stay firm and plump.

Set the cormels in a bag of just-barely-damp sand and next spring—just two weeks before planting-time—moisten the bag and place it in a warm room. Plant the cormels in the nursery the first year, and they will be ready for border planting by the second.

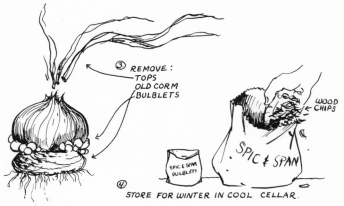

As soon as the weather turns cold, next spring's hardy annuals—larkspur, petunias, California and Shirley poppy, bachelor's button, alyssum, candytuff, snow-on-the-mountain, nicotiana and pinks—can be sown. Unless you have snow all winter, do not sow too soon—the seeds may germinate prematurely.

Azaleas can be moved now or at any time until late next spring. Be sure not to plant them any deeper than where they originally grew and take a good-sized rootball when digging them up. If some of them show a brownish tinge, they may have had too much sun; try relocating them in a somewhat more shaded spot.

Southern gardeners should also lift and divide their Easter lily bulbs if they have not already done so. This is also the time to prepare flats for seeding annuals and perennials including calendula, delphinium, pansy, viola and hollyhocks. Add equal parts of sand and finely-screened compost to well-pulverized soil, and fill the flats when the mixture has dried.

Roses and other woody ornamentals can be ordered and planted as soon as they are dormant in Zone Four southward.

Monthly feeding of roses should be resumed south of Atlanta. Rich manure, while excellent as a mulch, should be supplemented with fish fertilizer, cottonseed meal or blood meal.

In the South, in order to obtain the largest possible end bloom, you should stake, tie and disbud dahlias and chrysanthemums, using your thumbnail to nip off all the side buds.

Now's the time, out in the central states, to move the peonies that have been getting too much shade from competing trees and therefore producing fewer blooms. The soil of the new beds should be enriched with wood ashes and bone meal, and plants with buds should be set no lower than two inches below ground level. Mulch the surface of the soil with manure, but do not permit it to come in contact with the plant roots.

Gardeners in the Southwest can disbud their chrysanthemums now, giving them plenty of water, plus an occasional booster of manure water or liquid fish fertilizer which should be applied only when the soil is damp—never dry. Wash off any aphids that appear with a thin stream of water from the hose. Pansy and delphinium seeds (make sure the latter are fresh when you buy them) may be started now in the cold frame.

Out on the West Coast, lift and divide the spring- and summer-flowering perennials as soon as the fall rains start. Again, be generous with compost and rock fertilizers when preparing the new growing spots. The roses in the coastal gardens should also be given booster waterings and mulching and, as they go into the fall spectacular show, encourage them with extra cottonseed, blood meal or fish fertilizer.

This is the best month for planting daffodils or narcissus. Take care to give each bulb plenty of room because it divides in two just about every year—in two years four bulbs will live in the same space you now are giving to a single one. At the same time, start pansy seeds in the cold frame; you'll have some cheerful plants to work in among the daffodils.

When the tuberous begonias show signs of slackening off, allow them to go somewhat dry. Wait for another month or so to pass—when the stalks drop—before digging the tubers.

Deadline for seeding lawns is September 20th north of the Bluegrass Line and September 10th in Zones One and Two. Spread an inch of screened compost over established lawns in all areas. In Zones Five and Six sow ryegrass over Bermuda, carpetgrass, centipedegrass or zoysia to keep the lawn green over the winter. This operation may be done next month in Zone Seven.

To prevent leaves from matting on the lawn which can be harmful, rake into large piles which should be circled with wire fencing to keep them from blowing away. Make the heaps and piles as large as you conveniently can—Stanley Bulpitt advises that a five-foot-high pile of leaves will probably compost itself without any more help from you. The trick is to make a five-foot-high pile on your own home grounds.

Oak leaves should be composted separately for use next spring on the azaleas, rhododendrons, andromeda and other heaths. If you have any aged leaf mold left over, mix it in with this year's leaves to help decomposition.

Take down, clean and paint all birdhouses, replacing them in colder areas with winter roosting boxes. They are made like birdhouses, but have entrances at the floor level, and are equipped with perches above the entrances. Put up feeding stations and stock them when the snows arrive. Do not stop feeding the birds until spring because they will have come to depend upon your handouts for their survival. They are still your best allies in the never-ending war against our insect enemies.

The Orchard and Bush Fruits

Now's the time for residents in Zones Four through Six to put their orders in for the fruit trees and bushes that will be planted as soon as they are dormant. If he's close enough, pay your nurseryman a visit so you can select and reserve your plants.

It's a very sound practice to get your planting holes ready well in advance so you can get your trees and shrubs in them with as little delay as possible. Meanwhile, set a definite date on which the nursery will dig up the trees and shrubs and present them to you. With a working schedule like this your plants will suffer as little transplanting shock as possible.

Remember also to have plenty of compost and rock minerals on hand when you are ready to transplant. Handled this way, the new trees and shrubs will suffer as little shock as possible and be ready to make a good start in the spring. Some nurserymen advise that after planting, a daily watering until the ground freezes hard encourages extra root growth and a stronger plant.

Rock fertilizers should be spread now around Zone Two and Three berry bushes, trees and grapevines. If you've got the time and energy, drill holes around each plant under the dripline, and fill them with granite dust and rock phosphate. But until the frosts arrive and the plants are really dormant, go slow with the nitrogen fertilizers like bloodmeal, soybean and cottonseed meal. Eighteen-inch-long earth augers which fit in your electric drill are available, as well as water drills that can bore down three feet and fit on the end of your hoseline.

Fall care of your shrubs should include generous watering up until the time the ground freezes. This is important for the evergreens and also for the new plantings which are not too well established. If the weather is fairly dry in your area, you should water the shrubs and new plantings once a week.

Your evergreens and as many other varieties of trees as possible should be bought balled and burlapped. Remember to mix in as much peat moss and compost as you can spare in the planting holes and water generously. Once again, some nurserymen recommend a daily drenching up until hard frost because it makes for extra root growth. If you're in the habit of keeping your coffee grounds, pine needles and oak leaves separate, they'll come in handy as mulch.

Have you made any storage arrangements in the garage or cellar for the winter? The perfect storeroom is a frost-free cellar with a window, that's isolated from the oil burner or furnace. Apples and pears will retain the highest-possible percentage of their vitamin content if kept in a moist, well-ventilated cellar just over 32 degrees—but be sure to cool them quickly after they are picked.

Remember that gases given off in the ripening of pears and apples tend to speed the process, so be sure to ventilate the storage rooms at night while temperatures are low. Also, keep humidity high by sprinkling the floor with water to prevent fruit shrinkage. Proper temperature and humidity will not only help preserve the quality of the fruit but its vitamin content as well.

Be careful not to spoil your apples with over-hasty picking before the leaf-green color has left the skin. Red fall apples should have a ground color of yellow-green. If yours are not coloring properly, snip a few leaves out of the way so they are more exposed to the sun.

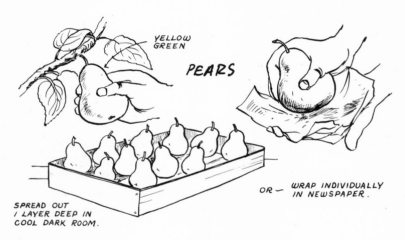

However, pears should be picked as soon as the leaf-green skin tone lightens to yellow-green—they should be picked before they are dead-ripe because tree-ripened pears tend to be gritty. After picking, spread them out one layer deep in a cool, dark room. Seckels are an exception—they must be russet-brown to be ripe and ready to pick.

Quinces should be allowed to ripen on the bushes for another month before they are harvested. They are judged ripe when their aroma is noticeable 50 feet away and their flesh is golden while their bloom is lavender-gray.

In Zones Three and Four, grapes should be picked for storage before they are entirely ripe. Allow them to develop their full sugar content in a dark, cool room. But for the best table flavor, let them hang on the vine until they are ready to drop when touched. However, you may lose a lot of them to the wasps, so be prepared to protect them either with netting or paper bags. Pears and grapes should be stored in trays in single layers. For long storage, pears can be wrapped individually in newspaper.

Apples can be stored in bushel baskets if they do not bruise easily like such "keepers" as Jonathans, Rome Beauty, Northern Spy, Winesaps, Northwestern Greening, Yellow Newtown and York Imperials. Next time you order trees, keep these varieties in mind. Northern Spy and York Imperial are very rich in vitamin C, while Rome Beauty, Jonathan and York Imperial are good pollinators. Easily bruised varieties that take extra care in handling include Yellow Transparent, McIntosh, Melba and Duchess.

Remove all boxes, cartons and baskets from the orchard at the end of the harvest. Look for and destroy any codling moth cocoons you may find. Rock fertilizers should be spread now around berry bushes, trees and grapevines in Zones Two and Three. If you've got the time and the two-inch soil auger that fits in your electric drill, you can drill holes around each plant's dripline and then fill them with rock phosphate and granite dust, watering them in. But go slow with the nitrogenous fertilizers like cottonseed, soybean and blood meal until the frost arrives and your plants are really dormant. In addition to the 18-inch-long soil auger, you can work with water drills that bore three feet down and fit on the end of your hose.

Under Glass

If you started your winter vegetables a month or two ago or are busy doing so now, it might be good to keep in mind that transplanting dates to the greenhouse fall just about now. This applies to tomatoes seeded in June and July, lettuce that you began last month and that will continue well into the winter, radishes that should be seeded every 14 days from

November through March, and cucumbers that were begun in August and should be transplanted in September. Onions can be started from sets.

Recommended varieties for the greenhouse are as follows: tomatoes—Floralou, Manapal, Michigan-Ohio Hybrid and Tuckcross O. Indoors; Bibb lettuce; Burpee Hybrid cucumbers; Beltsville Bunching and Sweet Spanish onions.

For all this activity you'll need plenty of compost, sifted topsoil, rotted manures, leaf mold and potting soil mixtures. These should be stored in bins—we use 50-gallon containers— in the garage or garden house where they will stay moist and not leach out.

The tomato plants, especially, should be moved indoors now in Zones One through Three as the nights turn cool. A good-sized plant will require a five-gallon container—galvanized pails are fine—placed where it will get the most light. Night temperatures should not fall below the 60- to 65-degree mark, so be prepared to add some extra form of light and heat.

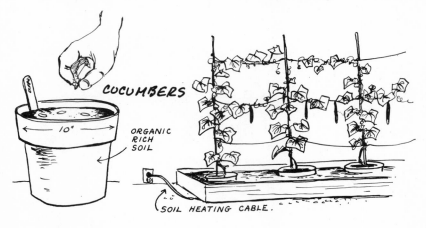

The winter radishes as well as the lettuce and spinach, should be sown in the hotbed or in greenhouse flats. It's time to lift and pot chives, basil, rosemary and parsley for an indoor supply with fresh flavor. But be sure to keep them outdoors in the shade for one more week before moving them to the windowsill.

Cucumbers, for best results, should be grown in a warm house with a minimum night temperature of 60 degrees. Sow in large eight-to-10-inch pots in soil that's rich in organic material—well-rotted sheep manure is excellent, if you can get it. Thin to six to eight inches apart if sown in benches, and provide a trellis or strings for the plants to climb. A soil-heating cable four to five inches down, running a 60-to-65-degree temperature should be used in houses that are cooler than 60 degrees.

Vacation is over in Zones One through Four for the pampered house plants that summer out of doors in favored spots. But before bringing them in, check their root systems for overcrowding or being potbound. Repot when necessary, using plenty of compost in the mixture. Make sure inside ventilation is adequate, especially during the first week. You're also advised to check all plants for garden pest infestation before bringing them in; don't hesitate to quarantine any dubious plant that could infect the other greenhouse residents.

Among the first to be brought in will be the gardenia and marantas. But as the nights turn increasingly cooler, more and more plants will return to the windowsill, leaving only the hardy chrysanthemums and spring bulbs.

If you set them immediately in an indoor planter filled with peat moss, these windowsill plants will best get over the shock of coming back inside. So be sure to thoroughly wet down your fall supply of peat moss for your winter planters. After soaking, arrange the pots in the planters, and fill in the spaces between them with damp moss.

Be generous and use a fresh supply of moss; anything left over from last year should be put to use in the garden. This is the way to get rid of your indoor pests which cannot survive for long outside.

Late-blooming chrysanthemums can be delayed by giving them an hour or two of light late at night. But if you want your poinsettias to bloom in time for Christmas, keep them all away from any lights that might fall on them after sundown. Both operations—lights for the mums and darkness for the poinsettias—can be achieved simultaneously by making an opaque cage cover for the latter.

Many of your border plants can be wintered in the greenhouse. Annuals that are perennials in warmer areas will live over and bloom next spring earlier than new plants grown from seed. Make cuttings of coleus, impatiens, fibrous-rooted begonias and shrimp plant while discarding the older plants that are now overgrown in the border.

While the tulips can wait until next month, the daffodils and narcissus should be potted now for spring forcing. Plunge the pots into an open cold frame and cover them with three inches of straw. But be sure not to cover the frame until the nights are really frosty; the potted bulbs need rain to help them form new roots.

Anemone corms may be started this month or the next in a rich, fibrous soil mixture with equal parts of sand, peat moss or leaf mold. Grow in flat or deep bulb pans, pressing the corm down so that it is covered with at least two inches of soil. Water thoroughly and set in a protected cold frame until late November or December. If the weather is not too cold in your area, they may stay in the frame until January.

Annuals that may be seeded this month for greenhouse growing include African daisy, snapdragon, bachelor button, candytuft, cineraria, winter marigolds, nasturtium, sweet peas and torenia. Perennials that may be sown include columbine, gaillardia, pampanula, the hardy carnations, delphinium, dianthus, foxglove.

Make cuttings now of plants for traditional Christmas gifts —African violet, begonia, dieffenbachia, dracena, gloxinia, geranium, ivy, peperomia and philadendron.

Before the weather gets really cold make a final check of all electric soil cables and of greenhouse heating units. Go over the glass, inspecting it for any putty shrinkage and loosening that may have developed over the summer. Apply new weatherstripping and caulking compound before cold weather arrives and makes the job harder.

October
Frost
and Your
Late Garden

It feels like frost was near—
...The spring was late that year,
But the harvest early.

Ridgely Torrance

"Hurry," she says, "or we'll lose the tomatoes."

Hurry? It's 4 in the morning, and since you like to sleep under blankets with the window open, not all the frost is outdoors under the glittering gaze of Taurus the Bull and the great Jupiter—your breath is plainly visible in the bedroom.

"Hurry," she repeats patiently, rising from under the covers without a shiver, "we'll have to cover the tomatoes."

143

And such is the power of her word and the purity of her dedication to the garden, that you follow her stumbling-blind in the dark—"Don't turn on the light; you'll frighten the neighbors"—out to the shed where the baskets and hotcaps are stacked neatly against this emergency.

Undeniably it has come on a hard, fast frost; so hard and fast that the air can't drop fast enough from our hillside into the hollows and low places around the highway and town. Enough of it remains in our little patch to nip our late-comers and chill their vitality from tip to stem to root.

So into place the covers go, over and around our last precious crops, with maybe a bit of hay and straw here and there, where it will do no harm and perhaps a little good. Shivering, intent and quiet, we work against the coming of the dawn, and when our dogs raise their throated alarms, they are answered, by every 4-footed guardian in the township, or so it seems.

And then, suddenly you are through, either out of hotcaps or plants, and it is permitted you to retire decently from the field of valor—your hillside vegetable patch—to your place of refuge, the once-warm bed high up on the third floor, just under the sloping slate roof.

However, naturally and contrary-wise, you choose to linger. "When did you last see the sun come up?" you banter as, hand-in-hand, you stumble along the rows and middles until you come to the potatoes which you planted in straw and leaves. By now it's quite obvious that more mulch is needed, so back to the shed you go while the woman of the house stands vigilantly in wait, a formless bulk in quilted corduroy.

And so you while the time away until the sun has come up, and it's back you go, this time to the kitchen where you feel, for a change, that you have honestly earned your flap-jacks, maple syrup and coffee.

You've saved the tomatoes from the first hard frost of the season and watched the sun come up not far from Pleasant Valley.

What's the average date for the first killing frost in your area? If you're not sure, you'd better consult the frost date map inside the rear cover which is based on the years 1899 to 1938. In our part of eastern Pennsylvania we're right on the October

10th-October 20th line, while southern New Jersey which is a bare 25 miles below us, enjoys ten additional days of garden safety—until October 30.

Your interest in frost and what it can do to your remaining crops should obviously be more than academic at this time, and the old-time gardener has learned by now to keep a watchful eye on the thermometer and to stand ready either to harvest his last crops or to protect them as best he can.

So we piled bales of hay around the tomatoes which we covered over with old storm windows. And, late at night, we sallied forth to cover up the individual plants with baskets and any hotcaps we had handy, and then draped lengths of burlap, retired curtain material, blankets, carpeting—what-have-you—they all went over the midnight rows. Most of the time they worked, or we said they did.

By now it's no secret that farmers and gardeners anxious to extend production and put the land to work, have consistently planted crops in regions where they are not used to growing—it's too cold. And, since frost—check the map again—occurs in practically every section of the country, low-temperature damage is a gardening problem all of us have to face; no zone is absolutely safe, except for the very southern tip of Florida.

But we have help from the plants themselves, which should enable us to garden both wisely and safely. The cold-hardy vegetables have "learned" (Is it because they evolved near the edges of melting glaciers?) to develop cold resistance within their tissues. Nobody knows for sure just how they do this trick, but cabbages can survive ice formation within their leaves, and we've picked field-salad in January after brushing away the snow that covered it.

If you'd like to know about the cool-region crops that prefer 60 to 65 degrees and are able to stand up to freezing weather they may meet up with in the field without injury, here's a list of cold hardy vegetables that may or may not relieve your mind about your garden's chances: cabbages and related plants including Brussels sprouts, kale, turnips, rutabagas, kohlrabi, collards, sprouting broccoli and horseradish; also spinach, beets and parsnips.

Then there are the plants—tender annuals included—that are able to survive in areas where the thermometer sags well below the freezing point, by completing their life cycle, from seed to seed, during the period between frosts. The herbaceous perennials die back on top, but maintain life well below the ground level in their roots, bulbs and tubers. Down there they are protected from freezing and subjected to much less cold. Also, among the half-hardy varieties, coverings of snow or leaves give considerable protection from low temperatures and therefore permit them to survive even prolonged periods of severe cold.

From the really frost-resistant types we proceed—and this is where all of us are vulnerable—to the cool-season crops that can be damaged by freezing. They include heading broccoli and cauliflower, lettuce, carrots, celery, peas and potatoes. If you have these in the garden, it would be sound practice to pile up bales of hay, baskets and hotcaps so you'll have them handy on one of those days when you can just smell the wet, cold leaves and know that, starting at 4 p.m., the temperature's going to fall two or more degrees an hour.

Logically, the list of plants that will stand a chance of survival in adversity should end here. But gardeners are not logical, so here's a list of crops that are tolerant to frost, but prefer temperatures that range from 55 to 75 degrees: all onions, garlic, leeks and shallots. Plants that are tolerant neither to frost nor to prolonged exposures to cold include: muskmelons, cucumbers, squash, pumpkins, all kinds of beans, tomatoes, corn and some varieties of peppers. Finally there are the warm-region, long-season plants that will not thrive below a temperature of 70 degrees: watermelons, sweet potatoes, eggplant, okra and some varieties of pepper.

But, take courage! If you can protect the more sensitive vegetables in your garden from the first light frost or two, they will usually continue to grow and yield for several more weeks. Tender plants such as the tomatoes and eggplants, are generally damaged when the mercury stands at 30 to 32 degrees for several hours, particularly when the sun comes up bright and warm the next morning. The half-hardy crops, however, can survive even when the temperature falls to 20 degrees.

So, ready those portable cold frames, and dust off the hotcaps. And bear in mind that sagacious old adage that appeared in the 1941 *Yearbook of Agriculture*: "Natural protection (of plants) is frequently supplemented in farming by practices such as mulching."—Enough said!

The Vegetable Garden

① POT CLUMPS OF CHIVES FROM GARDEN.

② STORE IN COLDFRAME FOR CHILLING PERIOD -

③ BRING POTS IN TO SUNNY WINDOW IN SUCCESSION FOR USE IN SALADS AND FOR COOKING.

Harvest the sweet potatoes as soon as they have been touched by frost. After the first freeze strikes, cut the tops from the roots early in the day to prevent the bitter juices from going back into the tubers. In Zone Four, late in the month, the fall planting of white potatoes can be ready for harvesting.

At this time gardeners in Zones Two, Three and Four should spread manure on the rows where they intend to plant early peas next spring. Although there will be some loss from leaching, turn the manure under, but leave the earth rough and then cover with straw to prevent erosion. You'll be able to plant your peas during a premature thaw by pulling the mulch to one side and making a shallow furrow for them.

While the Jerusalem artichokes should have formed tubers, dig only enough for your immediate use. As soon as the soil has a frozen crust, mulch the bed with a thick layer of leaves. This will prevent hard freezing and allow you to dig up the tubers at any time. You can do the same with carrots in all but the coldest areas.

If you find your artichoke tubers have shrunk in size, it's time to make a new bed. Transplant some to a bed of rich soil that's deeply dug, and set them 18 inches apart.

It can be a challenge—and a rewarding one!—in Zone Seven to take a chance on a "good" winter—you never can be sure! —and show beans, eggplant and tomatoes for very early crops. Portable cold frames will give you extra insurance if the weather goes bad, or if your area is not entirely frost-free. As we noted last month, they don't have to be expensive; the double-facing frames, high in the middle and tapering down on both sides, can handle two rows at a time.

Sheet compost should be worked into empty beds in Zones Four, Five and Six before the fall rains start. Cover cropping is a good habit if your soil is sandy or needs extra building up. This practice tends to keep the nutrients in the upper soil layers and prevents leaching down beyond the root systems of next year's crops.

Strawberry beds in Zones One through Seven should be taken care of now. Spread straw or boughs over the bed as soon as the ground freezes in Zones One and Two. These same materials should be collected and held for future use in Zones Three and Four. In Zones Five, Six and Seven, the beds are best planted at this time. Prepare the soil well with plenty of rich compost, mulch the plants generously as soon as they have set, but do not allow them to develop blossoms before spring.

Southwest gardeners should continue to set out cabbage family plants like broccoli, cabbage and cauliflower. Edible-podded peas as well as the telephone variety should also be planted; chives and parsley can be sown in the herb garden. Mulch light, and water well when there is a hot spell.

Fall plants of white potatoes may also be ready for digging in Zone Four later in the month.

Sheet compost should be worked into empty beds before the fall rains start in Zones Four through Six. A cover crop, however, may be advisable if your soil is on the sandy side. This will use the available food in the upper soil layers and store it up for next year so it does not leach out beyond the roots of the coming crops.

Cut the heads from the sunflowers before the seeds ripen thoroughly so they do not mould or shatter. Cut them on a dry, sunny day, and hang in an airy place to complete drying.

Divide and reset the rhubarb roots now. Each mature, well-grown plant should provide you with three or four new plants.

Watch tomato plants in Zone Four southward for outstanding wilt-resistant specimens. Be sure to save a fruit from each for seeds.

Check the "Under Glass" section and coordinate. Dig and pot enough herbs from the vegetable and herb patches to fill the kitchen windowsill this winter. Clumps of chives dug and potted now should be chilled in the cold frame with the spring bulbs which are to be forced. The chives may be brought indoors in succession to provide a series of young shoots for winter salads. In addition, marjoram, parsley, lavender, rosemary and oregano can be wintered on an unheated sun porch. However, these may not survive a winter outside in Zones One through Three.

Your leaf bins and wired enclosures should start to be filled now. Make it a point this year to appropriate all the leaves in your neighborhood that would otherwise be burned. Find out if your town delivers leaves or permits your loading up at the town dump—municipal officials are usually only too glad to have you do this. If you have the time and equipment, shred the leaves before storing them—with just a little patience a rotary mower does a first-rate job, bouncing the masticated leaf particles in a steady stream off a handy wall. Next year you'll have a good supply of leaf mold because the shredded particles break down faster than the whole leaves. If you plan to compost the leaves without shredding, remember that Stanley Bulputt recommends stacking them in piles at least five-feet-high and five-feet-wide—eight-feet-wide and eight-feet-high is most effective, he tells us.

The Ornamental Garden

In Zones One and Two mulch peonies with rich manure as soon as the ground freezes. Also be sure to cover the rock garden with evergreen boughs as soon as the cold weather settles in. The branches will serve to anchor the snow which is essential to the health of the Alpines.

Dig up the tender corms and bulbs as soon as they have been frost-bitten, and store tropicals such as Peruvian daffodils, in a warm cellar; the dahlias and glads will be better off in the cool cellar. Hang them bulb-down until the tops dry. Then they should be removed with excess soil from the bulbs, and bury them in baskets filled with sawdust or perlite.

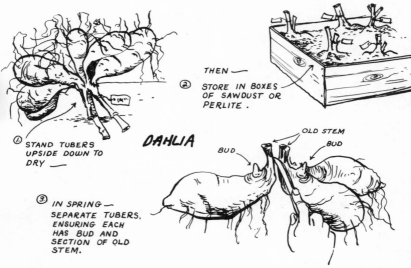

① STAND TUBERS UPSIDE DOWN TO DRY —

② THEN — STORE IN BOXES OF SAWDUST OR PERLITE .

DAHLIA

③ IN SPRING — SEPARATE TUBERS, ENSURING EACH HAS BUD AND SECTION OF OLD STEM.

BUD   OLD STEM   BUD

It is generally best to leave last year's corm attached to the gladioli until spring-planting time when it will separate easily. Handle the dahlias with care, leaving the clumps entire when you can separate them with one shoot to each section. Dig the Peruvian daffodils, cannas and tritoma, each with its clump of soil, and be sure to store so the soil does not dry over the winter. A large, perforated pliofilm bag for each clump is excellent. Dig and dry out tuberous begonia corms after the first frost strikes.

As soon as they are finished blooming, prune all the late-flowering shrubs. Cut back the roses in Zones One through Three, and mound or otherwise protect tender varieties. Do not feed roses in Zones Four through Six, but give them water unless rain is abundant in your area.

Further west, perennials such as iris, day-lily and coral bells may still be divided. It's good practice to mulch the shallow-rooted plants thickly to prevent heaving. If you take a spadeful of soil with each plant, chrysanthemums can be moved while in full flower—which gives you a good chance to re-arrange your color combinations.

Meanwhile, there's still time down south to start the winter-blooming annuals. Pansies, snapdragons, calendulas, and prim-roses may also be transplanted from the cold frame or lath house. Where they will bloom, random-sow the seeds of pop-pies, larkspur, scarlet flax and golden African daisies.

In Zone Six, bulbs including Dutch iris, narcissus, anemones and ranunculus, may be planted. Refrigerate the tulip bulbs for six weeks longer before you plant them. After you plant them, broadcast seeds of sweet alyssum, nemophia, creamcup or nemesia over the bed.

Rose bushes should be cut back half-way in the colder areas. Bend down the tops of tender tree roses, ramblers or climbing teas, and mount soil over them. When you're not sure about hardiness, lift and store doubtful varieties in a cold frame. Roses can be planted this month in Zone Five if you can obtain dormant plants, and beds should be prepared in Zones Six and Seven for mid-winter planting. Out on the Pacific Coast this is the best time for planting roses. Select a well-drained site, and prepare the soil at least two weeks in advance by digging bone meal, compost and peat deep into the bed and allowing it to settle.

In Zones Two to Four wherever snows cannot be relied on to last all winter, prepare to protect perennials as soon as a hard freeze comes. Salt hay or evergreen boughs, especially the latter, are recommended for delphiniums, primulas and oriental poppies.

In Zones Six and Seven, plant winter annuals now in the beds that were prepared last month. The hardy annuals includ-ing alyssum, phlox, baby's breath, bachelor's button, larkspur, petunias, hollyhocks, and Shirley and California poppies, should be the first to go in. After the cold weather is past, add such spring and summer annuals as marigolds, zinnias, torenias and other heat-tolerant species. Meanwhile, the summer-blooming perennials should be allowed to dry out in these areas.

As soon as your bulbs arrive, plant tulips in Zones One through Five. Give each bulb a generous handful of bone meal stirred into the bottom of each planting hole. If rodents are a problem, plant each bulb inside a tin can whose ends have been removed. Bulbs of the same variety, planted at the same depth, should bloom simultaneously. If you're working for a succession of bloom, vary the depth from five to seven inches. The shallower-planted bulbs will produce several small bulbs, each of which will reward you next year, but with smaller blooms. The deeply-planted bulbs will each make one new large bulb and will give you one large flower this year—something to look forward to.

Cut back the iris leaves to four-inch fans. Inspect the exposed tubers, and destroy any that are hollow—they harbor borers.

Continue to feed exhibition chrysanthemums until the buds show color.

If you have not already done so, plant Italian ryegrass over your Bermuda lawn. Sift an inch of screened compost over the old grass before planting, and rake it in with the seed.

Zone One and Two gardeners should mulch azaleas and rhododendrons with oak leaves.

Begonia tubers should be lifted on the West Coast, stored in trays of vermiculite, sand or peat moss, and kept cool until it's time to start them into growth in midwinter. Fuchsias can be cut back one-third, and stored in a cold frame. They should not be allowed to be completely dried, but should be kept very slightly moist until spring.

The Orchard and Bush Fruits

Orchardists in the central states should pull back the mulch six to eight inches from the trunks of fruit trees and grapevines. Put wire screening around the trunks of the younger trees to keep the rodents away from the tender bark. It's also prudent to plant some kind of "nurse" screening to protect young windbreaks until they are able to handle the winter wind.

All north-side plants should get burlap-and-frame protection from the rigors of winter. A good two-by-two frame will last for years if you make it durable, and cover it with a good grade of burlap. Some gardeners fill in the frame with leaves from top to bottom to give their plants real winter protection. If you can obtain them, use pine needles and oak leaves for the azaleas and rhododendrons.

As soon as they are completely dormant, fruit trees and bushes may be safely planted in Zone Four southward plus the warmer sections of Zone Three where winter temperatures do not fall too steeply. Residents in the colder areas should order now, but specify spring delivery.

Southern homesteaders can order their citrus and pecan trees now for January or February delivery. In the meantime, all tree and bush planters should prepare as much compost as possible for use on planting sites which should be dug now while the ground is workable. Remember that shredded leaves piled five-feet-high and five-feet-wide can be a good source of compost and mold next spring.

In the Southwest this is a good month to plant the hardier evergreens—trees and shrubs. But hold off working with the tropicals until next spring unless you are quite confident that your area is frost-free. Keep the deciduous trees and shrubs well-watered, although they are without leaves—to keep their roots from drying out. However, it's wise practice to hold up on the irrigation of the more tender plants in order to encourage winter hardening.

Root cuttings of loganberries and blackberries can be taken this month. Permit the roots to callus over before you plunge the cuttings into the cold frame to sprout. Cuttings of pears, figs, grapes and pomegranates may be taken as soon as their leaves have fallen. They should be placed in cold frames or stored for spring planting. This is also a good time for making root cuttings of bramble-fruit bushes.

Trees should be entirely bare before they are dug for transplanting. The young trees in the home nursery should have their straggly roots cut back before planting, but the tops should not be pruned back until spring.

Unless your compost piles really heat up, don't try at this time to compost the infected and diseased fruit as well as the mummies from the orchard. Instead, dig a deep trench in the vegetable garden and bury all the fruit in it. But if you do compost, be sure to place the fruit in the hottest part of the pile.

Eggs of peach-tree and apple-tree borers may have been laid in the bark of your tree below the soil-line. These can be killed off by scraping the soil away from the top three or four inches of the main root and leaving it exposed to the cold. Eggs not killed off by the cold may be found in the spring by the birds before the borers have a chance to burrow into the bark. Examine the bark carefully next spring before replacing the soil.

As soon as the crops have been picked, remove all baskets, trays, ladders and other equipment from the orchard, and examine them carefully for codling moth cocoons before storing them for the winter.

Be sure to stake and guy-wire your young trees securely if you live in a windy area. A minimum of three wires is recommended, and be sure to apply plenty of old rags or pieces of old garden hose where you tie the rope.

Get out, clean up and install your homes and feeding stations for the birds. They'll reward you next year by keeping your place reasonably free of insect pests.

Under Glass

It may be a trifle early for tomatoes, but if you were foresighted enough to start a pair in oversized pots or planters in the garden, it's time to bring them in and give them a place where they'll get all the available sun. Be sure night temperatures don't drop below 60 degrees—65 is ideal—and be prepared later to light them artificially as the days shorten. Be sure to use incandescent lights if your fluorescent units don't produce the full spectrum on the red end.

The useful herbs—rosemary, oregano, and marjoram—all related, should be potted for winter storage and used in the cold frame or in the cooler part of the greenhouse. A windowsill is fine for basil, chives, mint and parsley in addition to garlic. Like tulips or narcissi, the chives should be forced before being brought indoors. Give them one or more months of outdoor chilling before moving them inside.

This is the time to start the winter greens and radishes. They call for a bottom heat of 65 to 70 degrees for germination and 60 degrees after that. Thinning will prevent damp-off and give you a few side trimmings for the table. It's also time for a second planting of greenhouse or hotbed lettuce. If you're not bringing in tomatoes from the garden, do the same for them by giving them a daytime seeding temperature of 75 degrees and a nighttime temperature of 60 to 65 degrees.

Roses will do well even in a cool greenhouse, if there is plenty of light—do not try to grow any if yours are shaded by trees or nearby buildings. Put new plants in ten- or 12-inch pots containing a mixture of equal parts of compost, peat moss, well-rotted cow manure and a four-inch potful of bone meal per bushel.

Water well, and place in a protected, deep cold frame or storage pit under at least 12 inches of straw or well-packed leaves until December. You can do the same with spring-rooted cuttings and older plants from the garden which have been cut back rigorously. Varieties which do well in the greenhouse include Garnet, American Beauty, Madame Herriot, Pernet, Pinocchio, Better Times, Sparta, Talisman and Vogue.

Although we have left our frost-hardy azaleas out in the garden to winter giving them plenty of protection and subsequently noting no damage, it is time before a heavy frost arrives to bring the more sensitive varieties indoors. Carefully check your own weather timetable because azaleas can stand a light frost which is said to aid in the setting of next year's buds. They should be watered sparingly until February to keep them from drying out and may be kept under a bench until then.

Almost all the windowsill plants should now be safely back in place. But don't let the sun's last hot rays damage the foliage you protected so carefully outdoors—if you gave it plenty of shade during the summer, set up a thermometer nearby so you can check the temperature. If necessary, mist-spray on the warmer days and give the foliage plenty of protection—rig up sheets and pieces of thin cloth so they stand between the plants and the sun.

The late-blooming annuals—calendula and petunias—may be potted and brought indoors now so they can bloom handsomely for several months if given a sunny window in a cool room.

Cuttings can be taken this month from fibrous-rooted begonia, flowering maple, broom, croton, the ivies and star-of-Bethlehem.

Before the last chrysanthemums are ready to open in their outdoor beds, cut and store some for your Thanksgiving table arrangement. Cut just as the buds start to open, strip off all the leaves and plunge the stems into deep pails of water. Store in an unheated garage or building away from the sun where cool but not freezing temperatures prevail; add to the water weekly until Thanksgiving. Trim an inch or more off the stems just before you arrange them.

Hyacinths potted from September through mid-November, will provide a succession of bloom beginning at Christmas. Use a sandy loam mixture enriched with bone meal—one four-inch potful to the bushel. Set single bulbs in a four-inch pot, three in a five-inch, or five in an eight-inch pot. Water heavily, and store in a deep storage pit or dark, cool cellar for three to four months. Place under a bench in the greenhouse until color appears; water regularly, and feed liquid manure water every ten to 14 days. Give full light exposure when color appears.

Daphne should be grown cool and watered sparingly until December, unless Christmas bloom is desired. To force for Christmas, keep it well watered and grow at 55 to 60 degrees.

Shift the ferns and other shade-lovers from the cooler to the rather warmer windows, and keep them there, October through March.

During the latter part of the month or early in November, bring in the winter-flowering pansies from the cold frame. Set in four- to six-inch pots in an equal mixture of compost, leaf mold and rotted cow manure. Water freely, keep moist and feed with liquid fish fertilizer (one tablespoon to the gallon) every two weeks. Keep in the lightest part of the greenhouse at 45 to 50 degrees.

An old-fashioned method of forcing that is still popular is working with hyacinths in a glass. The glass should be suitable for the largest bulbs. Fill it with water just short of the bulb, and store in a dark closet, cupboard or cellar until the leaf shoots are three to four inches long and the roots fill the glass.

Gradually bring the sprouted bulb into the full light, and grow in a sunny window, taking care, when watering, not to break the tender roots. Varieties which respond well to early forcing in December and January include Ann Mary, Bismarck, Delight, Jan Bos, La Victoire, Pink Pearl, Winston Churchill.

Now that you're bustling about, clean out the window boxes, and add compost to the depleted soil. The smaller evergreens show up well in boxes during the winter, and can be returned next spring to the shrubbery border. Get ready for the birds by setting up feeding stations—by this time we've cleared the petunias out of the back porch feeding boxes which are now filled with seed mixtures.

The days may be warm early this month, but the nights in Zones Two and Three will later turn cold with killing frosts. So keep an open eye for that sudden drop in temperature which can kick off automatic heating units. The self-regulating ventilators should also be checked to make sure they're working properly. Everything should be in order so it runs smoothly on the first cold night. So, check again. The roof and side ventilators may be safely open in the first part of the day, but prudently closed by the afternoon. Likewise, the cold frame should be opened each day until the permanent cold arrives, but closed at night.

November
Notes for November

Listen ... With faint dry sound,
Like steps of passing ghosts,
The leaves, frost-crisp'd,
Break from the trees and fall.

November Night
Adelaide Crapsey

As the earth in your garden cools, the earthworms retreat to the warmer areas further underground. They cannot remain near the surface because one or two degrees of frost will kill them. But they have been known to survive as many as ten winters, burrowing six or more feet down to hibernate.

Mulch on top of your soil can raise the frost line many inches. The thicker the mulch, the higher the frost line. If you want to keep your earthworms happy over the winter—mulch deep. But if you want to aerate the subsoil, leave the surface mulch thin, so the worms will burrow down.

When spring comes, the earthworm returns to the surface and, as the days become warmer, resumes his job of burrowing, tunneling, digesting and procreating. If your soil contains lots of humus—decomposing vegetable matter—the earthworms will live happily in it. But if humus is scanty, some worms will leave or die for lack of proper food.

The birds migrate chiefly to follow their food supply. The insect-eaters must go south when the insects go deep into the bark of trees or deep into the ground. The Canadian goose which eats roots and seeds, departs when the seeds and marshgrass roots are frozen in the mud.

The robins whose diet is more than 40 percent insects, generally fly to Florida or the Gulf Coast. But the phoebes and flycatchers go a little further, mostly wintering in Central America or Mexico. The hummingbird must go all the way to the rain forests of South America to find the nectar secreted by tropical vegetation.

Winter chilling is necessary to help apples, pears and peaches bear next year—possibly a "habit" they "learned" while being next to the glaciers for a couple of hundred-thousand or million years. But the chill must not come too suddenly, and the temperature during November should not drop too low, or the fruit buds may be killed. The buds harden best with a gradual, steady decline from October's cheerful frostiness to the zero days and nights of midwinter. This accumulation of hardiness is necessary. Properly tempered apples, American plums and sour cherries can stand cold to 30 degrees below zero, while pears, sweet cherries and Japanese and European plums can remain vital at 20 below zero.

Usually, in this country, these low temperatures are not reached when the soil has a cover of sod, a cover crop, mulch or—even—snow. But in a snowless, cold winter, deciduous trees growing in open soil can be killed from the roots upward. So if your fruit trees are growing in a bare, recently tilled orchard, spread mulch over their roots before the mercury plummets any lower.

Long before the Pilgrims held their first Thanksgiving dinner, harvest festivals were observed in this country. The ancient Peruvians worshipped the "Mother of Maize" and attempted every year to persuade her to again bring in a good harvest.

Among the North Dakota tribes, the corn spirit was known as the "Old Woman Who Never Dies." She was believed to live somewhere to the south, and each year she sent migratory birds—her ambassadors—to watch over the crops. Dried meat was accordingly set out on scaffolds for the birds, and when the birds flew south in the fall, they were thought to take the meat back to the "Old Woman" who would reciprocate by remembering the tribe favorably the next year.

In Austria, a doll made from the last sheaf of grain cut in the field was called the "Corn Mother" and was carried home in the last wagon. The finest ears from the last sheaf were set in a wreath of flowers and then presented to the head farmer or placed in the village square by the prettiest girl harvester.

In upper Burma when rice has been piled in its husks on the threshing floor, the friends of the household are invited to the barn for a feast. Food and drink are placed upon the heap of rice, and an elder prays to the "Father and Mother" of the paddy plants for a good harvest next year. Then, just as we do, the whole party celebrates this year's crop with a feast acknowledging—just as we must—that human efforts are responsible only in a small way for the success of the year's harvest.

Happy Thanksgiving!

The Vegetable Garden

Winter vegetables in Zones Two through Four—carrots, parsnips, leeks, Jerusalem artichokes—should be covered with a thick blanket of leaves as soon as the ground begins to freeze. We've used our row-long cages to hold the leaves in place, but flat rocks will do just as well—you can also use newspapers if you've got other uses for the leaves. While you're about it, mark the rows with fairly tall stakes just in case the snow is heavy this year.

In Zones Five through Seven, plant a few nursery-grown, frost-proof cabbages now. If you'd rather start the cabbages from seed, sow the seeds two weeks before your first expected frosts which should occur about November 10-20 in Zone Five, and from November 30 to December 10 in Zone Six, and December 20 in Zone Seven.

In Zones Six and Seven continue planting winter spinach, onion sets, rape greens and English peas. Pick the winter vegetables as they mature, replanting them with hardy spring crops such as lettuce, carrots, cabbage and beets. Sow seeds in the cold frames for winter salads, and prepare to start melons, cucumbers and squash under glass next month for February transplanting. In Zone Five, plant lettuce and cabbage seeds, and cover the beds with a coarse mulch of twigs or pine boughs as soon as the seedlings appear. When you uncover them in the spring, you will have some hardy and promising young growths for early transplanting.

Now's also the time in the really frost-free areas to plant potatoes, tomatoes, beans and eggplant. You should also start preparing that asparagus bed where you plan to set out asparagus roots next month. Double-spade it, apply lots of rock fertilizer, and compost.

It's time to clean up the vegetable patch going north from the Bluegrass Line. Get the crop residues out of the ground and into the shredder, combining them with leaves plus the contents of the family garbage pail. In the compost pile you can layer this mellow mixture with great success against your early spring plantings.

Then give the pile a final fall turning, and cover it against heavy rains and snow. Heavy tarpaulins, carpeting or plastic are all good. If you can do it, a permanent roof is best because it also shades the heap from the sun during the rest of the year.

But Zone Three and Four residents who find that their soil is still workable through Thanksgiving will do well to spread the shredded aggregate in the now-empty rows and till it under thoroughly, adding manure and rock fertilizers. Finally, cover the tilled rows with a two-inch layer of shredded leaves, and you'll be all ready for next spring without any further ground preparation.

Winter vegetables such as carrots, parsnips, leeks and Jerusalem artichokes should be covered with a thick blanket of leaves as soon as the soil begins to freeze. Hold down the cover with old burlap and rocks, and place stakes to mark the rows when they are covered with snow.

Salad greens that are growing out in the open should be protected by sunshades. These include hardy escarole, corn salad and endive all of which will last much further into the winter if the sun does not reach them too early in the morning after a cold night. Evergreen boughs make a fine cover, but one-sided tents lined with burlap or muslin and facing the southeast, will also be first-rate. We used row-long wire frames or racks for years, pinning the necessary strips of cloth in a matter of minutes to achieve extra-long crops.

On the West Coast, gardeners should take full advantage of a dry period to prepare beds for the earliest spring planting. If turned under now and thoroughly mixed with the soil, fresh manure will be completely broken down and ready by early spring.

In the warmer areas winter vegetables can be picked as they mature, while the empty rows are replanted to lettuce, carrots, cabbage and beets. If you're in the habit of starting from seed, sow two weeks before the first expected frosts.

The Ornamental Garden

You might as well start digging a planting hole now for the live Christmas tree you're going to have this year. The ground should still be mellow and workable in all areas except parts of Zone One, so go down deep and wide and do a thorough job. Store the soil indoors while you fill the hole with straw or hay to keep it from freezing too far down.

At planting time—probably just after New Year's Day— water the tree well, and stake it securely against the wind. A burlap shield on the windy side should help it get through the first hard months. Last year in eastern Pennsylvania we followed this practice with complete success and hope to duplicate it once again this year.

Most lilies thrive and prosper best when planted in November. Give all varieties good drainage and rich soil, and follow the dealer's instructions regarding the planting depth and soil pH that they favor.

Perennials, except for the winter-bloomers, may be lifted and divided now in Zones Five and Six. The now-empty holes should be filled with lots of compost while plenty of fertilizer is dug into the new planting sites. Bone meal should be worked in around rose bushes, and the tender varieties should be hilled up protectively. While final pruning should be put off until spring, soft growth may be trimmed at this time.

Mound the soil one foot deep around the bases of the roses whose hardiness is suspect, and spread manure in the hollow between the mound. Protect the canes with a sturdy framework of one-inch-square wood, and stretch a sheltering sheath of burlap around the four posts to protect each plant. Fill the interiors with shredded leaves or chopped corn cobs or old, worked-out grass clippings. Climbing roses or rambler canes should also be checked and well-tied. They can be injured or bruised by whipping about in the winter wind.

Roses may be planted at this time out on the West Coast, particularly the vitamin-C-rich rugosas. And then there are the berrybearers to dress up the winter borders such as the cotoneasters, pyracantha, laurestinus and pernettya. Most lilies will do their best when planted at this time if given good drainage and a rich soil. Be sure to follow the advice of your supplier regarding pH and planting depth.

Gardeners in Five through Seven can plant holly, azaleas, camellias and other broad-leaved evergreens any time after the middle of the month right on through the winter. It's also time, later in the month to plant sweet peas in heavily-composted soil. Throughout most of this area, dahlias and caladiums should now be lifted—but even in the warmest parts they should be heavily mulched. As far north as Zone Three, it's still time to plant the seeds of hardy annuals so they will come up early next spring.

Cut back your chrysanthemums to the ground as soon as they have finished blooming. Make a rough diagram and check if any of the plants seem to be overcrowded, so you will be ready and able to dig and divide them next spring. It's also good to plan next year's display now by ordering the new varieties and colors that are advertised in your midwinter catalogs.

For this year's Thanksgiving bouquet, remove all leaves from the stems and then plunge them into a pail of water, leaving only the blossoms exposed on top. Store the cut flowers in your garage or cellar if the temperature stays safely above the freezing mark there. And be sure to move all the chrysanthemums that you feel are a little tender for your area, into the cold frame.

Lawns in the northern areas should be cut two-inches-long (or slightly more) and clippings allowed to accumulate as soon as growth stops. Bermuda grass lawns below the Bluegrass Line can be top-seeded with ryegrass. If the grass has already come up, but looks yellow, it may need an extra feeding of screened compost.

In Zones Six and Seven, tulip bulbs may be removed after they have been refrigerated for at least 60 days, and then planted. For the best results, set them eight to nine inches deep. Daffodils and amaryllis may also be planted now. Most lilies thrive and prosper best when planted during November.

Give all varieties good drainage and a rich soil, and follow the dealer's instructions regarding the recommended planting depth and soil pH.

Check your perennial bed for puddles after a long November rain—the standing water can kill many plants in winter. Dig a shallow trench that will lead the excess water away, and make a determined note to raise that bed come next spring.

November can be hard on your tender tropical favorites that are growing so far from their normal habitats. You'll be richly rewarded if you coddle them somewhat with wrappers from the frost until they get used to it. Bear in mind that the young plants are much more sensitive than their elders. So mound the soil as high as possible around your tropicals and subtropicals until they have come successfully through three up-north winters.

Be sure to work with soil that drains well—wet feet can be as bad for the plant as cold. Do not wrap any tender plant in an airtight covering because good ventilation is almost as good protection as extra warmth.

Clean the drains and gutters above evergreen and perennial plantings to prevent ice formation in the winter.

The Orchard and Bush Fruits

① V-SHAPED TRENCH TO TAKE WHOLE PLANT.

② COVER ENTIRELY WITH SOIL.

③ MULCH WITH STRAW WHEN SOIL IS FROZEN.

There's still plenty of time, the professional nurserymen assure us, to plan for late-fall planting of the newly-arrived dormant bare-root stock. Your holes should have been planted well in advance—wide and deep—and you should have plenty of humus, compost, leafmold, and topsoil on hand. Play it safe by working with aged manure so you avoid any chance of rootburn.

The same team of experts advises us to keep watching the newly-planted whips or trees right up until the first hard frost. They argue that the extra watering stimulates last-minute root growth although the rest of the tree is dormant. Stop watering when the ground freezes hard.

After planting, stake your trees out using three pegged ropes, and slip a protective wire mesh cylinder around the young trunk.

Make sure that all newly-planted fruit trees are well-tied and braced against the winter wind. Protect the tender young bark from chafing by slipping a cut length of old rubber hose over the rope where it supports the tree. Until they are six years old, pecan trees should be protected with spiral wrappings of overlapping burlap that extend to the crotch.

However if you feel—particularly in Zone Two and many parts of Zone Three—that it's too late for planting, heel the trees in a V-shaped ditch that's generous enough to take the whole plant. Set the roots at the bottom of the V, and cover everything with soil. Mulch with straw after the ground is frozen hard—not before—you don't want mice feeding on the buds.

Gulf Coast gardeners south of the Bluegrass Line can plant deciduous trees, vines and shrubs, and also move their woody plantings. Be sure to keep the tops in balance with the roots which suffer damage at this time, by careful pruning of branches. Further west, nitrogenous fertilizers such as cottonseed meal can be spread under deciduous trees when they show bare. Work the fertilizer well into the top of the soil, and cover with a generous leaf mulch.

When your woody plants are fully dormant, spread a layer of rich manure under them, and cover it immediately with straw, hay or wood chips. This will prevent the ammonia from escaping, and give the winter rains and melting snows a chance to leach it down where the roots can reach it. Be sure to leave a foot-wide well or depression around the trunks to prevent damage by rodents.

In areas where the temperatures don't fall too sharply or too low, winter pruning can be started as soon as the leaves fall. But in the colder areas wait until the coldest weather is past before pruning.

Start this month to scrape loose bark off old apple trees. Spread a tarpaulin or cover of newspapers under the tree to catch the parings which should then be burnt because they may be filled with codling-moth eggs. Do not start winter pruning at this time. Wait until the coldest weather is past because freshly-pruned trees are highly susceptible to winter-kill.

Blackberries and raspberries in the colder parts of Zones Two and Three should be protected against winter injury. An easy way to do this now is to bend the canes over to the ground and heap soil over them, removing this cover in the spring when the ground thaws. Give the berry bushes a good layer of wood chips, manure, sawdust or shredded leaves. Blueberries should have an acid mulch like oak leaves.

Papaws and persimmons are at their peak flavor after the frost has nipped them. If the persimmons are on the cold and shady side of a hill, try leaving the fruit on all winter—it will retain its flavor until late in the season.

Clear all fallen fruit and leaves before spreading a fresh mulch of leaves under the fruit trees and bushes. Compost the trees' own leaves, and put down as thick as possible a layer of clean leaves from your shade trees. Spread the cover beyond the branch tips out to the dripline, but leave a bare circle one foot wide around the trunks so the mice won't nest there. Weigh down the new mulch with large, flat rocks. This procedure is recommended for stone fruit trees suffering from gummosis.

Give the berry bushes a good layer of wood chips, manure, sawdust or shredded leaves. Blueberries must have an acid mulch—oak leaves or pine needles are fine—but the other woody plants are not so particular.

Muscadines in Zones Four through Seven can be planted within the next few months. Set one male plant in every third spot in every third row.

Make preparations in Zones Four through Seven to protect the subtropical trees and shrubs that are especially liable to damage from low temperatures. This applies particularly to the younger—up to two years old—plants. Draw the soil high around the avocado trunks and be ready to protect the citrus trees from the first frosts. Later in the winter, oranges can stand temperatures that might harm them this month.

Do something for the birds! Put out feeding stations and keep them filled, and space out some homes and houses in strategic areas. Make provision for both the small juncos and sparrows as well as the avaricious, bullying jays and starlings by installing at least two smaller stations. You'll have cleaner, pest-free orchards and home grounds next spring.

Under Glass

This is the last time in the greenhouse or hotbed to make lettuce plantings in time for use next March and April. It's also worthwhile trying your luck with onions and radishes. You should also tie your tomato vines to stakes, washing the foliage gently and frequently. You will probably have to use a toothpick with a cotton tip or a camel's hair brush to achieve pollination.

The salad greens started earlier should be earning their keep now, helping out at the table and enhancing the menu. Always take the largest plants when thinning the rows. Be sure to do a thorough job of thinning so there is no chance of overcrowding. Our carrots grew much straighter and longer after we worked the rows conscientiously.

Seeds that require stratification should be started at this time. Among these are many of the woody ornamentals and some perennial Alpines. Plant them in cold frames, separating the seeds according to the number of months or years they require for germination. Cover the surface of each bed (in which the soil has previously been pulverized and enriched) with a layer of perlite. For the smaller seeds barely cover the surface and make the planting layer twice as deep as the diameter of the larger seeds.

After sowing the seeds and gently, but thoroughly, moistening the bed, cover the surface with paper or burlap. Germination is most successful when the seeds are watered occasionally with tepid water and then buried under a cover of snow heaped inside the frame.

Cuttings of gardenias and fuchsias can be started with bottom heat this month. Cover the gardenia cuttings with glass jars until they root. This is also the time in the greenhouse to sow seed for snapdragons, candytuft, dwarf dahlias, clarkia, acrolinium and schizanthus for bloom indoors.

If your bulbs for forcing have arrived late, try to have them potted by the tenth of the month or Election Day. Nest the pots in a cold frame, and cover them with a thick layer of leaves. Hay, if you have it to spare, will also do. Be sure to label each pot and draw a diagram showing its position, if necessary. Cover the glass top with matting—old burlap bags, etc.—for extra protection.

Plants in the cold frame may require winter protection, so cover them with salt hay if you live near the coast; otherwise, use leaves, ordinary hay or straw. It's also a good practice to prepare for the really cold nights by setting in a supply of mats, straw-filled old burlap sacks, carpeting and what-have-you, to cover the frame and hotbeds.

While you're about it, this is the time to lay in an extra supply of burlap, blankets, old mattings, curtains, bedspreads, strips of linoleum and old carpeting against the sure arrival of the first cold night. They'll be put to work, covering your cold frames, hotbed and planters and should save some late crops and protect tender plants.

The extra cover performs two functions—it keeps the interior from heating up too much on the warm days, while reducing the chances of a freeze-up at night.

Just as you would in the garden, make a diagram showing the position of each clearly labeled and identified pot, so it can be easily located when it's time to remove it later in the winter. Use a short wooden or plastic marker when labeling; the long ones may be displaced when you removed the covering of hay or straw.

While you're working between the house and what remains of the garden, pot up a clump or two of Astilbe Japonica, and place it in the cold frame until January or early February.

To produce Christmas bloom in your azaleas, bring them in now from the cold frame, making sure they receive a minimum temperature of 60 degrees, and feeding them once every two weeks with liquid fish fertilizer mixed one tablespoon to the gallon.

If you want your calceolaria to bloom late in January or early in February, give it two to three hours of extra light daily for the next six weeks. Place it under 60-watt bulbs set two to four feet distant. August-sown seeds ordinarily produce blooms in April to May.

Narcissi will bring color, and sometimes fragrance, to your winter greenhouse if you plant them in early November—Election Day is again a good deadline—in a fibrous potting mixture that contains sand and peat moss, adding a four-inch potful of bone meal to each bushel of mix. Work with only top-quality bulbs with double or triple "noses" that have not been previously forced.

They may be grown in four-to-six-inch deep flats for cutting, placed as close together as possible with the tip barely protruding. Water well and place in a storage pit, a cool unheated cellar, or in a garden trench that is 16 to 18 inches deep and covered with straw.

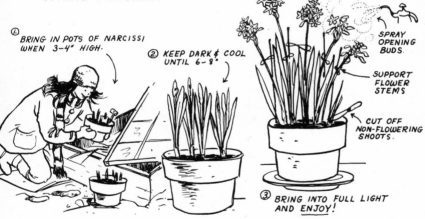

① BRING IN POTS OF NARCISSI WHEN 3-4" HIGH.

② KEEP DARK & COOL UNTIL 6-8"

SPRAY OPENING BUDS.

SUPPORT FLOWER STEMS

CUT OFF NON-FLOWERING SHOOTS.

③ BRING INTO FULL LIGHT AND ENJOY!

Bring them into the greenhouse when the leaf shoots are three to four inches long, and the flower buds are just visible. Late in December continue the practice by bringing in a pot or two of several varieties every ten to 14 days. Place the pots or flats under the bench until the leaves are six to eight inches long; then place them in full light on the bench, and water regularly.

Narcissi grow best at 50 to 55 degrees. The leaves and flower stalks should be supported with light rods or staffs and dark, soft string. When the buds open, spray them with a fine mist, and water the pots sparingly. Remove the foliage with a sharp knife if the side shoots do not bear blooms. When blooming is complete, cut off the dead flowers, but continue to water the plants until the bulbs can be transferred to the outdoor garden.

Indoors, it's time to move the more sensitive growths away from the windows, and check all sashwork for open cracks.

Bathe house plants frequently under running water, and be sure to quarantine any that may be infested with pests. Remove all virus-infected material immediately.

Most greenhouse plants will require less water during the next three months. Allow them to run somewhat dry during this period, unless they put on a display of winter bloom. Making sure your benches and walks are clean, damp down the walks and areas under the benches to keep humidity high.

Keep rotating plants in dimly-lit corners or on dark tables with those at the sunnier windows to keep them all in prime condition. Or, if it's possible, install a fluorescent bulb in the darker areas and keep it on during the day. Such kind treatment will be rewarded by most plants by putting forth a generous winter display of blooms that are long-lasting.

Wash any remaining whitewash off the greenhouse so you get full advantage of the low-slanting sunlight. During the coming short days, your plants will need all available light. While you're at it, clean off the benches and walks to avoid fungus troubles later on. The heating system should be working efficiently at this time. If the ventilators are automatic, check them once more to be sure they function properly during the sunny days that are followed by frosty nights. Remember to set poinsettias and other draft-sensitive plants in a sheltered area.

Ventilate the cold frames on sunny days, and do not allow the soil to dry completely. Examine all plants frequently, and quarantine any that are infected or infested. All plants that are virus-infected should be removed immediately, and the house fumigated with oakleaf smudge.

December
What Are Your Chances for a White Christmas

Are you dreaming of a white Christmas?

If you are, you'd better plan to spend it in northern Maine, Wisconsin, Michigan, Minnesota, the higher Rockies, the northern Cascades, or perhaps in Alaska.

If, on the other hand, you are the kind of an individual who prefers to sunbathe during the holidays, you can be almost 100 percent sure of a green Christmas within 250 miles of the Gulf of Mexico, in coastal California, in southern Arizona, and in Hawaii. But if you are young and athletic enough, there is a better than even chance that you may be able, on Christmas day, to ski in a bathing suit on new snow in the Sierra Nevadas, the Adirondacks, or perhaps in the Pennsylvania Poconos, thereby combining the benefits of both green *and* white Christmases.

What Are Your Chances for a White Christmas?

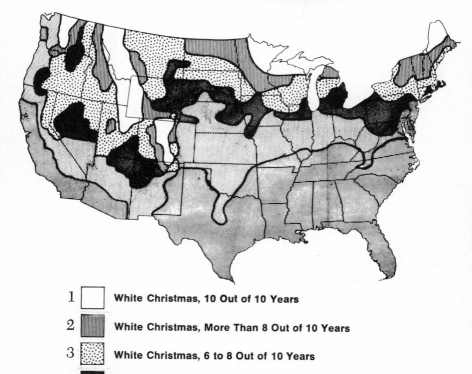

1 ☐ White Christmas, 10 Out of 10 Years

2 ▦ White Christmas, More Than 8 Out of 10 Years

3 ░ White Christmas, 6 to 8 Out of 10 Years

4 ■ White 4 to 6 Out of 10 Years

5 ▨ Some Snow in 1-4 Years Out of 10

6 ▥ A Green Christmas Without Snow

Our reckoning of white Christmas probabilities is based upon figures garnered from *Weekly Weather and Crop Bulletin* compiled by the weather bureau. The only figures, though, that can be relied upon with almost complete assurance are those for the green and white Christmases. Within memory of the weather bureau, the Southeast has always been green and the selected high points and northern spots white. But records are always being broken. No guarantees come with figures for this year.

Snow cover in many of the in-between areas may be spotty or nonexistent. For example, in the areas encircling the sure-fire white Christmas, snow is expected to cover about 90 percent of the ground 8 to 9 years out of 10. That's a pretty good chance, but it's only a chance. You might decide to spend the holidays in that cabin in the Maine woods where snow is almost a certainty, only to find that most of the white stuff is nesting in the pine canopy and very little of it has sifted through.

By Christmas time, snow will be no novelty in this country's highest mountains. It usually starts to fall in earnest by mid-October in the northern Rockies, though in some years, September sees the first inch that will stay on the ground. The Front Range in Colorado is usually covered by the end of October, and sometime in November snow comes to stay in most parts of Zones Two and Three. Merchants are often delighted by the first snows in Zones Four and Five, because they rev up the Christmas spirit by falling during the December Christmas shopping season and thus help attract large crowds of shoppers. Christmas sales in Zones Five and Six usually get no such boost, though snow may fall there between New Year's Day and the end of January, just to exasperate merchants and citrus-growers.

The date of the first snow is sometimes, though not always, an index of the amount that may accumulate during the whole winter. Total snowfall is more closely related to aridity and drought than to temperature in the fall and early winter. The depth of the snow in the western mountains varies from 50 inches to as much as 500 inches in a season; yet snow in the northern Rockies starts in early October and averages only about 200 inches, while in the Cascades, where snow falls a month or more later, it averages 400 inches. In Salt Lake City the first fall can be expected in mid-November, yet the total is only about 15 inches. Duluth sees its first flurries at the same time, but it piles up almost 60 inches. Portland, Maine, does even better, averaging 100 inches of fall throughout the winter.

Temporary summer drought or flood trends often continue to decrease or increase the winter's snow accumulations, too. In 1967 a weatherman at the Franklin Institute, Philadelphia, was asked what the chances were that the summer's heavy precipitation which could be affected by snow and drought, would continue into the winter. He hunted back through the records and found that in five out of six cases, a wet summer had been followed by a snowy winter, but a dry summer had been followed by a winter of scant snow cover. Drought-breaking rains deluged much of the Northeast in 1972 while the Ohio Valley states were drier than in the past 5 years. If the trend continues through the winter, Cincinnati's usual 20 inches of snow may not be forthcoming, but Philadelphia may pile up far more than its usual 20 inches.

The depth and duration of this winter's snow will affect your garden in a number of ways. Plant hardiness, for example, is dependent not only on the number of extremely cold days but also on the depth of the frost line which, in turn, can be affected by snow. Your groundwater accumulation can be partly determined by whether or not the soil freezes before the first snow. If the snow comes before the freeze goes deep, some soil organisms and tender roots may be able to live through the winter; if there is a heavy freeze first, they may die. It is interesting to compare the map above with our spring and fall frost crops which we have listed in the "Garden Calendar." These, taken in conjunction with the United States Department of Agriculture plant hardiness map which is based on winter temperature extremes, will explain much about the flora of any given area. Our gardens are dependent upon each of these factors, but where the snow comes early and stays late, it is possible to grow many plants which would die where snow cover is lacking.

An early and lasting snow that comes before the ground is frozen hard, blankets the surface to keep it open all winter. When the soil temperature is above freezing, the snow in contact with the soil melts steadily but slowly during the winter, and the water is absorbed by the soil without runoff, thereby increasing the amount of groundwater.

Clean snow melts little from the surface, even under a hot sun. Most of the sun's warm rays are reflected by the pure whiteness of a new fall, and they warm whatever is above the drifts. That's why skiers in high mountains where the sun is brightest through the thin air, are comfortable in light clothing, even in bathing suits. That is also one of the reasons why, at high altitudes, treetops are damaged so severely by alternately hot days and icy winds at night that their new growth dies each year, leaving the picturesque but deformed dwarfs we find up near the timberline.

If the snow is not very deep, the hot sun's rays can penetrate it to warm the black soil beneath, and to speed thawing from the bottom of the snow layer. Similarly, if snow gets dusty or sooty, the dirty cover absorbs the warmth, and the snow then melts from the top. That is one of the reasons why snow in a large city turns quickly to slush; and also why snow melts most quickly on a blacktop road; and why a layer of new snow melts more quickly if it has been deposited on top of a layer of dirty snow.

When soil is frozen hard before deep snow accumulates, watch out for runoff and floods to accompany the spring thaw! The Northern Plains are about the toughest areas to garden. There, the first freezes precede the first snows by as much as a month, and not only is the growing period there short, but temperatures dive to the lowest in the United States, and winter winds are brutal. Spring floods in the Mississippi Valley often have their source in the Plains States when sudden spring thaws and early rains melt the tops of the snowdrifts, and all the thaw water runs off because the soil is still frozen.

It would seem, from the foregoing, that it is desirable to keep winter temperatures of our garden soil as high as possible. How can we do this? The results of some soil studies indicate that the kind and number of trees on our property, as well as their placement, may help a great deal.

Flood studies made by the New England Regional Planning Commission show that 50 to 90 percent of a heavy snowfall may be intercepted by the treetops in a dense coniferous forest only to evaporate before it reaches the ground. Hardwood forests, being deciduous, accumulate most of the snow on the ground, little of it being held in the canopy. In the coniferous forest the ground freezes hardest and the sun penetrates least to warm it in spring before snow melt results in runoff. In the hardwood forest the soil is covered early with snow, winds are reduced and so is drifting; the soil temperature remains higher, and the accumulated organic debris beneath the trees absorbs large amounts of moisture when the snow melts, reducing runoff.

Organic mulch over our gardens in the winter acts much the same as forest litter. A ground cover, such as a winter cover crop, delays freezing somewhat and helps slightly to hold the snow, but is less effective than mulch. And if the mulch is deep and rough (like a thick layer of hay) rather than smooth and compacted (like a layer of leaves) it holds the snow best.

Properly placed windbreaks can also influence the winter temperature of your land. Not only do they shield your garden from the cold blasts, but they also prevent the snow's blowing off high spots in the garden where it is needed, to ditches and swales where it will only run away when it melts in spring.

To be avoided at all costs is the bare, plowed winter garden. Bare soil, it has been found, is coldest; coniferous dense cover is next; cover-cropped land comes next; then mulched soil; and warmest of all is soil under deciduous plantings.

The Vegetable Garden

It's a good idea for up-north Zone Two and Three gardeners to check their yearly records (if they have any) and the original garden plan for the year to see which varities produced best. The information you glean should come in handy when ordering your seeds for the coming year.

You should also be considering crop rotations for the new year because a good program will increase yields and eliminate disease carry-over in the soil. Remember that the bugs all-too-frequently lay their eggs in the soil where they find a crop they favor. If you put that same crop back in the same plot, you can have a fine infestation. So, change around wherever you can. A good, safe rule is to follow a root crop by a top crop, and vice versa.

The parsnips can be dug while the lettuce and radishes sown in the cold frame in September or October should now be ready for the table. However, the kale can be harvested, even when the heads are snow-covered. Cauliflower and radishes can go into the cold frame while the rhubarb should be mulched with well-rotted manure. Chicory roots—one of our best winter salad plants—can be grown in flats in the basement. Rhubarb may also be forced in the cellar or attic in barrels or boxes placed next to the chimney or furnace.

Depending on prevailing local conditions, the following vegetables may be planted this month below the Bluegrass Line: beets, cabbage, carrots, Brussels sprouts, cauliflower, Chinese cabbage, broccoli, collards, eggplant, endive, leek, lettuce, parsley, parsnips, rutabaga, spinach, Swiss chard, tomatoes and turnips. Be sure to apply plenty of compost when preparing the planting beds.

Florida gardeners can start the same crops suggested above with the addition of sweet corn. All young tropicals and seedlings should be protected with hotcaps, baskets or some form of cover when frost is predicted. Do not mulch the threatened plants because they may freeze and be killed more quickly with a mulch. (See comments and suggestions under "The Orchard.")

Radishes, lettuce and other greens may be planted in the hotbed in the upper South and in the cold frame further south.

Asparagus roots may be set out any time now up until next April 1. Double-spade the bed, filling the bottom of each trench with manure. After the new bed has been set, the spaces between the plants can be used next spring for quick crops such as lettuce, radishes and carrots—later cabbage. After the cabbages are out in the fall, cover the bed with a layer of coarse manure and give it over entirely next year to asparagus.

Further west and south, cover crops should be planted where vegetables cannot be started at this time. In other areas, the same crops suggested for the South may be planted with the addition of muskmelon and cantaloupe. Beds may be started for artichokes, asparagus and rhubarb, making them deep and enriching them with manure and plenty of compost. Old strawberry beds should be renewed now, and new ones started. While dormant, chives may be divided and filled in with parsley—both make good edgings for the vegetable beds. All planting should be well-watered and mulched to prevent frost damage.

Vegetables left in the garden in the Northwest should be mulched to prevent deep freezing of the soil. The tender crops such as lettuce, endive, parsley and spinach may be grown in the cold frame. It's good practice to heap up soil or leaves about the cold frame and put a mat or burlap bag over the top on very cold nights. A layer of barnyard manure over your beds will leach down over the winter, adding many valuable nutrients to the soil.

Gardeners in all areas are urged to clear all garden debris and crop residues now—if the job wasn't done at Thanksgiving. You'll cut down on insect hibernation and egg-laying by shredding all residues from the planting rows and patches. Add these to the compost piles or till them under together with a portion of your leaf crop. In general, get your garden as ready as possible for next spring's early planting of peas, radishes and lettuce.

The Ornamental Garden

Up in the chillier areas, winter mulches should be applied to many if not most plants, but only after the ground is frozen hard and deep. Half-hardy plants need a mulch over their root systems to prevent freezing although their tops may apparently die completely.

Place a light mulch on perennial and bulb beds and on all shrubs. Mulch the clematis vines with rotted manure and peat moss, and set a four-inch mulch of the new planting of bearded iris to prevent soil heaving.

Spread a generous layer of strawy manure over your peonies after the soil is frozen. Tender climbing roses should be removed from their trellises and carefully bent over to the ground. You may have to work slowly and carefully, in two or even three installments. Cover them with soil or ground corncobs. If the latter, you will owe the area an extra feeding of nitrogen next spring. Treat bramble fruits the same way in the coldest areas.

Tritomas should be lifted with the soil ball intact and stored in a cold frame or cool cellar. If you store them indoors, be sure to moisten them lightly once or twice over the winter.

If the ground is still open in your section, it is not too late to plant lilies and species tulips. This is also the month when you can sometimes buy Darwins or other hybrids at bargain prices. If you do buy, be sure to avoid shriveled or soft bulbs, and after planting, generously mulch those you buy so they have every chance to make roots.

As you pull up dead lily stems, keep a careful lookout for small bulbs at the end that was under the soil level. These can be planted immediately in the nursery and should provide plants that bloom in about two or three years.

Further south, it's time to plant such bulbs as amaryllis, Dutch iris, fritillaria and mariposa. Seedlings of sweet william, alyssum, candytuft, pansies, stock and calendula can be transplanted to their permanent sites, and the seeds of forget-me-not, California poppies, snapdragon, and sweet peas may be sown. Residents just south of the Bluegrass Line should rotary till the new flower beds and borders now, adding plenty of compost and bone meal, so they'll be ready for an early spring planting.

Florida gardeners should be ready to feed their poinsettias more fertilizer. Watch their leaves for telltale yellowing which means nutrients are lacking. The late-flowering lilies, callas, Dutch iris, dahlia tubers, glads, narcissus and Easter lilies should be planted this month. Amaryllis will especially benefit from a feeding of compost, bone meal and manure tea twice a month.

All young tropicals and seedlings should be protected with hotcaps and covers whenever frost is predicted. But do not mulch them—they will freeze and be killed more quickly with a mulch.

Past the Mississippi, there is still time further west and south to set out the hardy perennials and winter annuals. All plants should be well-mulched and watered. Use ample bone meal and compost in preparing beds for sweet peas and California poppies which should be sown for spring flowering.

Camellias may be planted from this time until February. Be sure to give them partial shade in hot areas, while in other places they will need temporary shade if planted in the full sun for the first two years. Camellias in all areas will need much more water if planted in the full sun than if they are shaded at midday. Stir large quantities of acid humus in the soil beneath them, but do not fertilize them until they have started into growth. Hose the foliage regularly.

Pinch stock and snapdragons back to encourage compactness, and stake and mulch chrysanthemums. Continue to plant gladiolus for successive bloom. If they have not done so already, gardeners in the Northwest should dig their tuberous begonias and dahlias now, storing them in a cool place in the sand. Tulips, iris and daffodil bulbs can still be planted.

Bulbs potted for forcing must spend nine weeks sunk in the garden or in a cold garage or cellar to make sufficient root growth. If you're working for successive bloom, bring in a few pots at a time.

Climbing roses in Zones Two and Three should be removed from their supports, and the canes laid on the ground and covered with soil. Bush roses should be hilled up for about one foot over the crown and then mulched. Tea roses may be laid on their sides, and covered with soil in the cold frame or dug up and buried in a trench lined with salt hay. New roses may be set out in Florida, while the established plants are fertilized heavily and given plenty of water. Further west, they shouldn't be planted until February, but now's the time to dig and prepare generous holes for them. Roses in the

Northwest should be given the same protective treatment as those in New England and the East—the climbers should be placed carefully on the ground and covered with soil. Christmas roses should be shielded with burlap or covered lightly with evergreen boughs to prevent damage.

The Orchard and Bush Fruits

MULCH WITH STRAW

PROTECT TRUNKS WITH WIRE MESH GUARDS.

OR — PAINT TRUNKS WITH REPELLANT.

TRAMPLE DRIFTS TO DISCOURAGE MICE.

First, don't forget to set up a Christmas tree for your bird population. Your assortment of sparrows, juncos, nuthatches—yes, even the starlings and jays—will reward you by keeping the homegrounds free of grubs and insects in the future. But now is the time to decorate a small evergreen or a slender deciduous tree with suet, sunflower heads and dried fruits. A cat-guard may be needed, and bribe the squirrels to keep away with an offering of nuts spread below. And, after the tree has been stripped, keep a steady supply of bird seed in your feeding stations, especially on the snowy days.

Trees and shrubs planted in the past season—the nurserymen tell us you can plant right up until the ground is frozen fast, hard and deep—should go into the winter with a good mulch over their roots to prevent heaving. Protect the trunks, especially on young fruit trees, with wire mesh guards that will keep the field mice and other rodents at a safe distance. Then apply a good, thick straw mulch weighted down with branches —good use for old Christmas trees.

If you're really plagued by rodents nibbling at tender young bark, you can protect your fruit trees by painting their trunks. The repellent is made of five parts resin melted into one part of linseed oil. Paint the trees well up above the expected snow line. Trample the drifts around each trunk after a snowfall to prevent the mice from tunneling under the snow.

Blackberries and raspberries in the coldest areas may freeze unless you protect them. Bend them to the ground and cover with soil or mulch.

In many areas further south this is considered the best time for planting trees—see comments above. Some of the most attractive ornamentals that can be planted in the south Atlantic states include holly, crape myrtle, sweet gum, tulip tree, magnolia dove tree, Franklinia, Carolina silverbell and Paulownia. In regions where the winter temperatures never go below 20 degrees, the orchid tree, pindo palm, the European fan palm, the hardy kumquat, fig, loblolly bay and Formosa rain tree may also be planted.

And if you live in the warmest zones, you will want to grow your own organic oranges. Order the trees now for a January or February planting. Four trees, two navels and two Valencias, will keep you supplied the year round. If you live anywhere near a nursery, visit it and pick your trees before they are dug—that's the best way to make sure you get first-quality stock.

Should you be a newcomer who has just moved to the South from the more rigorous northern areas, you'll have to make a few changes in your gardening technique regarding winter care. Don't mulch tender plants to protect them from the frost—they'll be more susceptible to winterkill if you do. Cover them instead with hotcaps—it's hard to beat the old bushel and half-bushel baskets—when frost threatens. You should also protect young trees when frost threatens, though the older members of the same varieties will go through light frosts without damage.

It's time to set out hardwood cuttings now in the home nursery. Many of them will develop enough roots to rate transplanting to a permanent site in the spring.

Central states residents should dig up roots of blackberries, raspberries and other bramble fruits for root cuttings. Choose roots one-quarter to one-half-inch thick, cutting them into two-to-four-inch segments. Bury in a cold frame in sand, or place under a greenhouse bench. After they have sprouted in the spring, transplant to the nursery row. Next winter they will need protection from the cold, but will be ready for the garden the following spring.

Plan a windbreak for next spring where the wind damage is greatest. In places where the snow cover is thin, a twiggy hedge can act as a snow tray when set in just the right position. In deciding the best angle and position, experiment now with movable barriers to obtain the best effects.

Winter pruning can be started as soon as the leaves have fallen in the Southwest. Where very low temperatures can be expected, wait until the coldest weather is past before starting. This pruning should be a lighter operation than the one that comes later because the trees don't replace the cut wood. Content yourself with the absolutely necessary pruning— damaged limbs and bad breaks.

Prune grapes and make cuttings now for propagation in the Southeast areas, setting the cuttings in nursery rows to root. New muscadines may be planted this month or the next, setting one male plant in every third site of every third row. You can determine and separate the light from the dark fruits by the color of the tendrils. White or scuppernong vines have light green tendrils; the black muscadines come from vines with bronze or reddish tendrils.

Holly is best planted any time from now until May. Choose the species that is best suited to your locality. English holly, which produces fine Christmas berries, thrives in areas where the temperatures seldom fall below ten degrees or rise above 100. Dahoon is even more tender. On the other hand, American holly is hardy all the way north to Boston.

Nurserymen strip the leaves from the plants when planting them, and prune back some of the branches as well. Plant hollies in groups, if you want berries. Some of the plants are male, others female, and both must be planted to produce offspring.

In the milder parts of the Northwest, fruit and nut trees may be planted, with one eye on the weatherman, where ground conditions permit. Pruning of both trees and shrubs should be completed this month. Remove dead canes of blackberries, raspberries and loganberries, and prune the grapes. Mulch all late-planted material, and stake all tall plants. The new plantings may need protection with burlap or heavy paper.

Under Glass

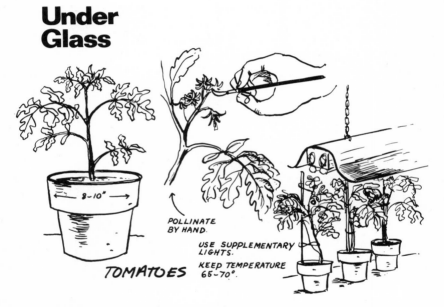

POLLINATE BY HAND.

USE SUPPLEMENTARY LIGHTS.

TOMATOES   KEEP TEMPERATURE 65-70°.

8-10"

Keep an eye on the cold frames and hotbeds. Are the electric cables working properly in the latter, responding to the thermostat settings? We find our thermostats overcompensate, so we set them about five degrees too low in order to achieve a 65-70 degree inside temperature. This can be important to your leaf lettuce which can stand—even prefers—moderately low temperatures.

The cold frames should be watered and ventilated on the warmer days. The potted bulbs that have been stored in the frame or under the benches in the greenhouse should be examined now. Start to bring in those whose roots fill the pots—a few each week—to prolong the period of bloom. Place them in a sunny window, and water them sparingly at first until they start to show signs of top growth.

Unless your outdoor tubs and planters contain really hardy specimens, bring them in to winter over in the cool basement or garage. If you leave the evergreens outdoors, be sure to give them plenty of water. Inside they need only enough to keep them from going bone dry. You should be on your guard not to water the house plants too much at this time and not to give fish fertilizer feedings until the days grow longer.

At the kitchen window start alfalfa seeds for salads and trimmings now. You can harvest them once a day or even more. Soak overnight to start, and thereafter keep moist but not submerged. Rinse daily in fresh water. You can keep your family in vitamin-packed greens all winter long by working with two glass baking containers, alternating them from start to harvest. But don't neglect your lettuce, radishes, chives and garden cress—they'll be needed later.

Your indoor-started tomatoes should be big enough now to go into eight-to-ten-inch pots. Lacking bees and insect visitors —and probably a good thing too!—you'll have to practice your expertise in hand-pollination. Use a camel's-hair brush or a cotton quill "Q" tip applicator. To achieve really productive growth, you will have to install lights to supplement the thin winter sunlight. Be sure to work with wide-spectrum fluorescent lights or add an incandescent bulb to give you the benefit of the red end of the spectrum. Finally, don't let night temperatures fall below 60 degrees—65 to 70 is ideal.

Liquid manure is the best plant food for the greenhouse. Where it is limited, we favor liquid fish fertilizer which is mixed one tablespoon to one gallon of water. But if you have a warm barn or toolshed and have an old barrel or 50-gallon galvanized can—fine. Fill the barrel or container half-full, hang a half-bushel burlap bag inside and let it soak. After ten days, add another 25 gallons of water. Always water early in the greenhouse—night dampness can bring on fungus.

Cuttings of evergreens, taken now, will make extra plants in the spring. Just before the New Year bring in the azaleas and hydrangeas from the cold frame for forcing. Start tubers now of the gloriosa for very early spring bloom, and pot Easter lilies late in the month.

Christmas gift plants may find it hard to survive for long in overheated, dry interior atmospheres, so it's up to us to make our home more like a greenhouse. First, you can add to the humidity by setting the plants on trays of moist sand, gravel or perlite, and mist-spraying them with water at least once a day.

Avoid high temperatures as much as possible because these plants have become accustomed to a cool greenhouse environment. Water them liberally—most of them are heavily rooted and wilt easily. Caladium bulbs require rich soil and plenty of water, with some morning or afternoon sun. But beware of overwatering your cacti and succulents, most of which are resting now. Also, Christmas terrariums and dish gardens have no drainage holes, so be careful when watering.

Exercise care when ventilating because direct cold drafts can cause considerable damage. Play it safe by opening the sashes on the side of the house away from the wind.

Sharing your plants with others is commendable, particularly at Christmas time, but great care should be exercised when moving your gift plants out of the greenhouse and then taking them out-of-doors to their new home or homes. Your begonias, kalanchoe, poinsettias and solanum—all quite susceptible to cold—require the extra precautions.

Carefully wrap each plant in layers of newspaper—10 to 20 sheets—if the weather is freezing outside, and warm up the car before bringing the plants into it. If you don't take these commonsensical precautions, the plants may reward you in a few days by dropping their leaves and displaying bare stems. It is obviously poor judgment to have this happen to plants which you otherwise tended so carefully.

Index

Average Dates of
First Fall Frosts

Zone One August 30 Zone Four October 20-30
Zone Two September 10-20 Zone Five October 30-November
Zone Three September 30 Zone Six November 20
Zone Seven December 20